Table of Conte

Table of Contents

Vocabulary: Beginning and Ending Sounds

Directions: Use the words in the box to answer the questions below.

ax	mix
beach	church
class	kiss
brush	crash

Which word:

begins with the same sound as **breakfast**
and ends with the same sound as **fish**? _____

begins with the same sound as **children**
and ends with the same sound as **catch**? _____

begins and ends with the
same sound as **cuts**? _____

sounds like **acts**? _____

begins with the same sound as **coconut**
and ends with the same sound as **splash**? _____

rhymes with **tricks**? _____

has **each** in it? _____

Name: _____

Vocabulary: Sentences

Directions: Use a word from the box to complete each sentence. Use each word only once.

ax	mix	beach	church	class	kiss	brush	crash

1. Those two cars are going to _____ .

2. He chopped the wood with an _____ .

3. Grandma gave me a _____ on my cheek.

4. Before you go, _____ your hair.

5. How many students are in your _____ at school?

6. The waves bring sand to the _____ .

7. To make orange, you _____ yellow and red.

8. On Sunday, we always go to _____ .

Vocabulary: Plurals

A word that names one thing is **singular**, like **house**. A word that names more than one thing is **plural**, like **houses**.

To make a word plural, we usually add **s**.

Examples: one book — two book**s**   one tree — four tree**s**

To make plural words that end in **s**, **ss**, **x**, **sh** and **ch**, we add **es**.

Examples: one fox — two fox**es**   one bush — three bush**es**

Directions: Write the word that is missing from each pair below. Add **s** or **es** to make the plural words. The first one is done for you.

	Singular	Plural
	table	_tables_
	beach	_____
	class	_____
	_____	axes
	brush	_____
	_____	crashes

Name: _____

Vocabulary: Spelling

Directions: Circle the word in each sentence which is not spelled correctly. Then write the word correctly.

1. How many clases are in your school? _____

2. Our town has six chirches. _____

3. Have you been to Maryland's beechs? _____

4. Water mixs with dirt to make mud. _____

5. We need two axs for this tree. _____

6. That car has been in three crashs. _____

7. She gave the baby lots of kises. _____

8. I lost both of my brushs at school. _____

Name: _____

Vocabulary: Nouns and Verbs

A **noun** names a person, place or thing. A **verb** tells what something does or what something is. Some words can be a noun one time and a verb another time.

Directions: Complete each pair of sentences with a word from the box. The word will be a noun in the first sentence and a verb in the second sentence.

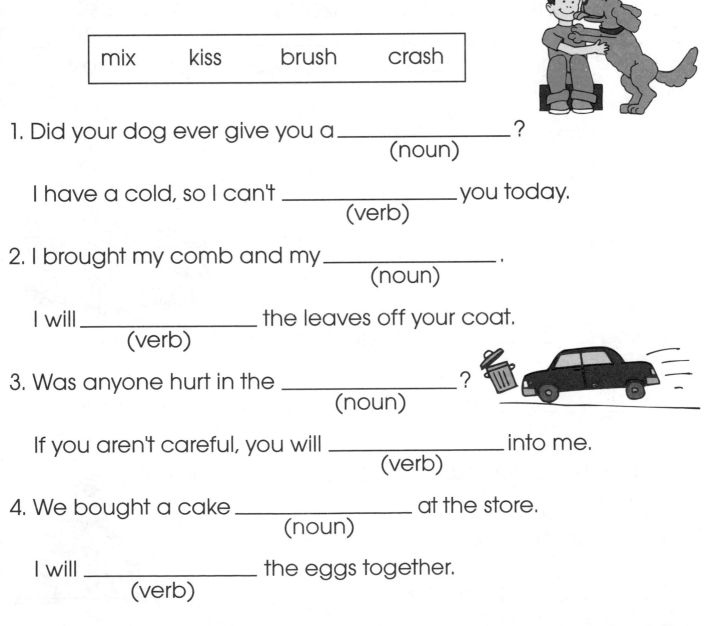

| mix | kiss | brush | crash |

1. Did your dog ever give you a _____?
   (noun)

   I have a cold, so I can't _____ you today.
   (verb)

2. I brought my comb and my _____ .
   (noun)

   I will _____ the leaves off your coat.
   (verb)

3. Was anyone hurt in the _____?
   (noun)

   If you aren't careful, you will _____ into me.
   (verb)

4. We bought a cake _____ at the store.
   (noun)

   I will _____ the eggs together.
   (verb)

Name: _____

Vocabulary: Nouns and Verbs

Directions: Write the correct word in each sentence. Use each word once. Write **N** above the words that are used as nouns (people, places and things). Write **V** above the words that are used as verbs (what something does or what something is).

Example:

I need a __N drink__ . I will __V drink__ milk.

mix	beach	church	class	kiss	brush	crash

1. It's hot today, so let's go to the _____ .

2. The _____ was crowded.

3. I can't find my paint _____ .

4. Will you _____ my finger and make it stop hurting?

5. I will _____ the red and yellow paint to get orange.

6. The teacher asked our _____ to get in line.

7. If you move that bottom can, the rest will

_____ to the floor.

Vocabulary: Sentences

Every sentence must have two things: a **noun** that tells who or what is doing something and a **verb** that tells what the noun is doing.

Directions: Add a **noun** or a **verb** to complete each sentence. Be sure to begin your sentences with capital letters and end them with periods.

Example: reads after school (needs a noun)

Brandy reads after school. _____

1. brushes her dog every day

_____

2. at the beach, we

_____

3. kisses me too much

_____

4. in the morning, our class

_____

5. stopped with a crash

_____

Review

Directions: Write one sentence about each picture. Write **N** above the noun in each sentence. Write **V** above the verb in each sentence. Be sure to spell any plural words correctly.

_____

_____

_____

Name: _____

Vocabulary

Directions: Find the picture that matches each sentence below. Then complete each sentence with the word under the picture.

list

spill

search

pound

toast

load

1. I will _____ until I find it.

2. Be careful you don't _____ the paint.

3. Is that _____ too heavy for you?

4. They made _____ for breakfast.

5. Please go to the store and buy a _____ of butter.

6. Is my name on the _____?

Name: _____

Vocabulary

Directions: Find the picture that matches each sentence below. Then complete the sentence with the word under the picture.

hug	plan	clap
stir	drag	grab

1. She will _____ where to go on her trip.

2. _____ that big box over here, please.

3. My little brother always tries to _____ my toys.

4. May I help you _____ the soup?

5. I like to _____ my dog because he is so soft.

6. After she played, everyone started to _____ .

Name: _____

Vocabulary: Word Puzzle

Directions: Look at the pictures below. Write the consonants they begin with on the lines. Then add vowels to spell words from the box.

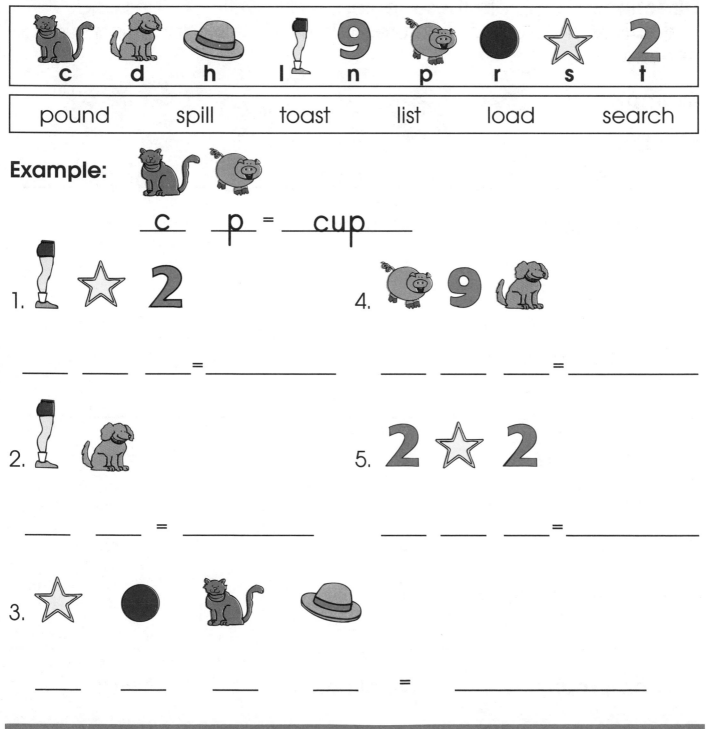

c   d   h   l   n   p   r   s   t

pound   spill   toast   list   load   search

Example:

     c   p =   cup

1.   4.

___ ___ ___ = _____   ___ ___ ___ = _____

2.   5.

___ ___ = _____   ___ ___ ___ = _____

3.

___ ___ ___ ___ = _____

Vocabulary: Adjectives

Adjectives are words that describe nouns. They often tell what kind, how many or what color.

Directions: Complete these sentences by writing nouns and adjectives. Then draw a picture to show what is happening in each sentence.

Example:

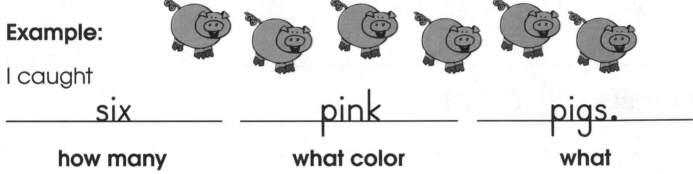

I caught

six	pink	pigs.
how many	**what color**	**what**

1. One day I hugged

how many	**what color**	**what**

2. My brother dragged home

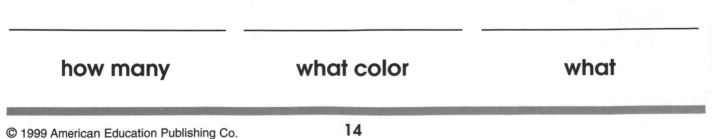

how many	**what color**	**what**

Name: _____

Vocabulary: Beginning and Ending Sounds

Directions: Write the words from the box that begin or end with the same sound as the pictures.

stir	clap	drag	hug	plan	grab

1. Which word **begins** with the same sound as each picture?

2. Which word (or words) **ends** with the same sound as each picture.

_____

_____

_____

_____

_____

_____

_____

_____

_____

_____

_____

_____

Name: _____

Vocabulary: Explaining Sentences

Directions: Complete each sentence, explaining why each event might have happened.

She hugged me because _____

_____.

He didn't want to play with us because _____

_____.

We planned to go to the zoo because _____

_____.

I grabbed it away from him because _____

_____.

We clapped loudly because _____

_____.

Vocabulary: Verbs

Directions: Write the verb that answers each question. Write a sentence using that verb.

stir	clap	drag	hug	plan	grab

Which verb means to put your arms around someone?

_____

_____

Which verb means to mix something with a spoon?

_____

_____

Which verb means to pull something along the ground?

_____

_____

Which verb means to take something suddenly?

_____

_____

Name: _____

Vocabulary: Past-Tense Verbs

The past tense of a verb tells that something already happened. To tell about something that already happened, add **ed** to most verbs. If the verb already ends in **e**, just add **d**.

Examples:

We enter**ed** the contest last week.
I fold**ed** the paper wrong.
He add**ed** two boxes to the pile.

We taste**d** the cupcakes.
They decide**d** quickly.
She share**d** her cupcake.

Directions: Use the verb from the first sentence to complete the second sentence. Add **d** or **ed** to show that something already happened.

Example:

My mom looks fine today. Yesterday, she _____**looked**_____ tired.

1. You enter through the middle door.

   We _____ that way last week.

2. Please add this for me. I already _____ it twice.

3. Will you share your cookie with me?

   I _____ my apple with you yesterday.

4. It's your turn to fold the clothes. I _____ them yesterday.

5. May I taste another one? I already _____ one.

6. You need to decide. We _____ this morning.

Vocabulary: Past-Tense Verbs

When you write about something that already happened, you add **ed** to most verbs. For some verbs that have a short vowel and end in one consonant, you double the consonant before adding **ed**.

Examples:

He hug**ged** his pillow.   The dog grab**bed** the stick.
She stir**red** the carrots.   We plan**ned** to go tomorrow.
They clap**ped** for me.   They drag**ged** their bags on the ground.

Directions: Use the verb from the first sentence to complete the second sentence. Change the verb in the second sentence to the past tense. Double the consonant and add **ed**.

Example:

We skip to school. Yesterday, we ___skipped___ the whole way.

1. It's not nice to grab things.

   When you _____ my cookie, I felt angry.

2. Did anyone hug you today? Dad _____ me this morning.

3. We plan our vacations every year. Last year, we _____ to go to the beach.

4. Is it my turn to stir the pot? You _____ it last time.

5. Let's clap for Andy, just like we _____ for Amy.

6. My sister used to drag her blanket everywhere.

   Once, she _____ it to the store.

Name: _____

Vocabulary: Past-Tense Verbs

When you write about something that already happened, you add **ed** to most verbs. Here is another way to write about something in the past tense.

Examples: The dog walked.   The dog was walking.
              The cats played.   The cats were playing.

Directions: Write each sentence again, writing the verb a different way.

Example: The baby pounded the pans.

The baby was pounding the pans.

1. Gary loaded the car by himself.

_____

2. They searched for a long time.

_____

3. The water spilled over the edge.

_____

4. Dad toasted the rolls.

_____

Name: _____

Vocabulary: Past-Tense Verbs

Directions: Write sentences that tell about each picture using the words **is, are, was** and **were**. Use words from the box as either nouns or verbs.

| pound | spill | toast | list | load | search |

_____

_____

_____

_____

_____

_____

_____

_____

21

© 1999 American Education Publishing Co.

Review

Directions: Read the questions below. Then write an answer to each question.

Pam's brother just won a singing contest. Pam and her family were watching. What do you think Pam and her parents did next?

_____

_____

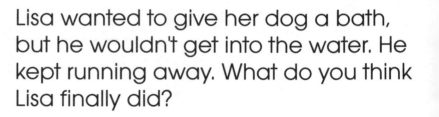

Lisa wanted to give her dog a bath, but he wouldn't get into the water. He kept running away. What do you think Lisa finally did?

_____

_____

Review

Directions:

1. Read the sentence below. On another sheet of paper, write the rest of the story. Use **is**, **are**, **was** and **were** with some of your verbs.

2. Read your story out loud. Are your ideas clear? Did you leave anything out? Make any needed changes and copy your story again.

3. Draw a picture to go with it.

4. Read your story to your family and show them your picture.

Sometimes eating with my family is full of surprises. One day . . .

_____

Draw your picture here:

© 1999 American Education Publishing Co.

Name: _____

Vocabulary: Present-Tense Verbs

When something is happening right now, it is in the **present tense**. There are two ways to write verbs in the present tense:

Examples: The dog **walks**.   The cats **play**.
                    The dog **is walking**.   The cats **are playing**.

Directions: Write each sentence again, writing the verb a different way.

Example:

He lists the numbers.

He is listing the numbers.

1. She is pounding the nail.

_____

2. My brother toasts the bread.

_____

3. They search for the robber.

_____

4. The teacher lists the pages.

_____

5. They are spilling the water.

_____

6. Ken and Amy load the packages.

_____

Name: _____

Vocabulary: Sentences

Directions: Write a word from the box to complete each sentence. Use each word only once.

glue	enter	share	add	decide	fold

1. I know how to _____ 3 and 4.

2. Which book did you _____ to read?

3. Go in the door that says " _____."

4. I will _____ a yellow circle for the sun onto my picture.

5. I help _____ the clothes after they are washed.

6. She will _____ her banana with me.

Name: _____

Vocabulary

Directions: Follow the directions below.

glue	enter	share	add	decide	fold

1. Add letters to these words to make words from the box.

   old _____   are _____

2. Write the two words from the box that begin with vowels.

   _____   _____

3. Change one letter of each word to make a word from the box.

   food _____   clue _____

4. Change two letters of this word to make a word from the box.

   beside _____

Name: _____

Vocabulary: Statements

A **statement** is a sentence that tells something.

Directions: Use the words in the box to complete the statements below. Write the words on the lines.

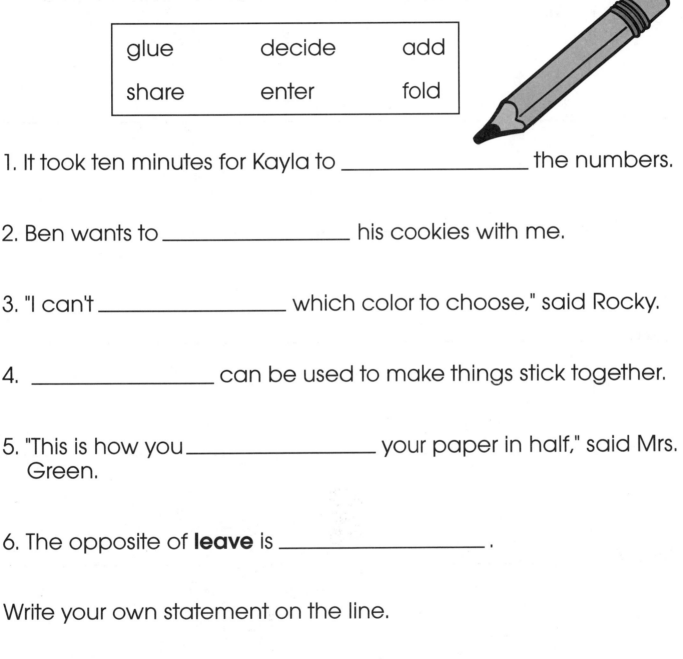

glue	decide	add
share	enter	fold

1. It took ten minutes for Kayla to _____ the numbers.

2. Ben wants to _____ his cookies with me.

3. "I can't _____ which color to choose," said Rocky.

4. _____ can be used to make things stick together.

5. "This is how you _____ your paper in half," said Mrs. Green.

6. The opposite of **leave** is _____ .

Write your own statement on the line.

_____

Vocabulary: Questions

Questions are asking sentences. They begin with a capital letter and end with a question mark. Many questions begin with the words **who, what, why, when, where** and **how**. Write six questions using the question words below. Make sure to end each question with a question mark.

1. Who _____

2. What _____

3. Why _____

4. When _____

5. Where _____

6. How _____

Name: _____

Vocabulary: Commands

A **command** is a sentence that tells someone to do something.

Directions: Use the words in the box to complete the commands below. Write the words on the lines.

glue	decide	add	share	enter	fold

1. _____ a cup of flour to the cake batter.

2. _____ how much paper you will need to write your story.

3. Please _____ the picture of the apple onto the paper.

4. _____ through this door and leave through

   the other door.

5. Please _____ the letter and put it into an envelope.

6. _____ your toys with your sister.

Write your own command on the lines.

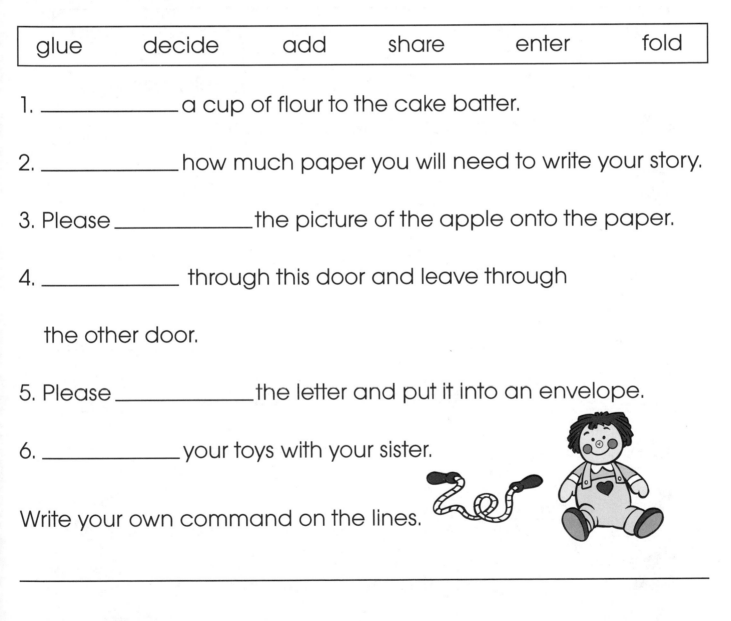

_____

_____

Name: _____

Vocabulary: Directions

A **direction** is a sentence written as a command.

Directions: Write the missing directions for these pictures. Begin each direction with one of the verbs below.

glue	enter	share	add	decide	fold

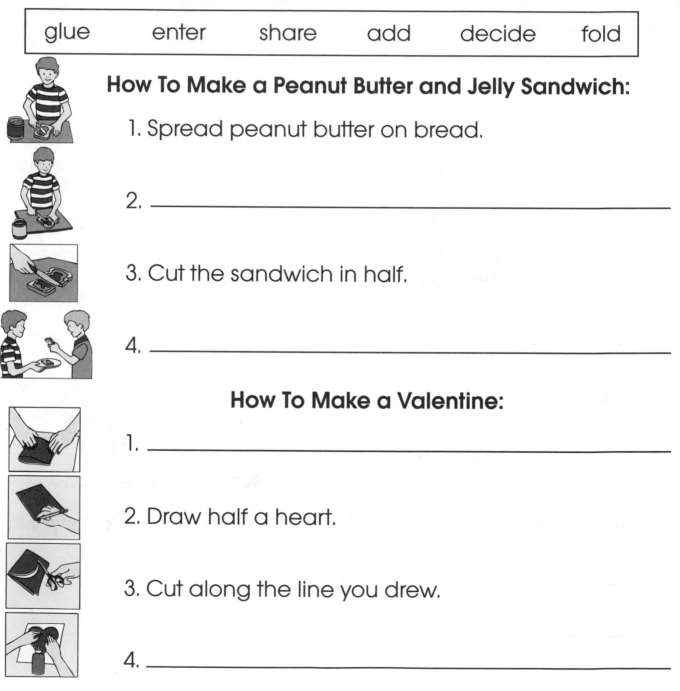

How To Make a Peanut Butter and Jelly Sandwich:

1. Spread peanut butter on bread.

2. _____

3. Cut the sandwich in half.

4. _____

How To Make a Valentine:

1. _____

2. Draw half a heart.

3. Cut along the line you drew.

4. _____

Name: _____

Kinds of Sentences

A **statement** is a sentence that tells something.
A **question** is a sentence that asks something.
A **command** is a sentence that tells someone to do something.

Commands begin with a verb or **please.** They usually end with a period. The noun is **you** but does not need to be part of the sentence.

Example: "Come here, please." means "**You** come here, please."

Examples of commands: Stand next to me.
Please give me some paper.

Directions: Write **S** in front of the statements, **Q** in front of the questions and **C** in front of the commands. End each sentence with a period or a question mark.

Example:

_____C_____ Stop and look before you cross the street.

_____ 1. Did you do your math homework

_____ 2. I think I lost my math book

_____ 3. Will you help me find it

_____ 4. I looked everywhere

_____ 5. Please open your math books to page three

_____ 6. Did you look under your desk

_____ 7. I looked, but it's not there

_____ 8. Who can add seven and four

_____ 9. Come up and write the answer on the board

_____ 10. Chris, where is your math book

_____ 11. I don't know for sure

_____ 12. Please share a book with a friend

Name: _____

Kinds of Sentences

Remember: a **statement** tells something, a **question** asks something and a **command** tells someone to do something.

Directions: On each line, write a statement, question or command. Use a word from the box in each sentence.

glue	share	decide
enter	add	fold

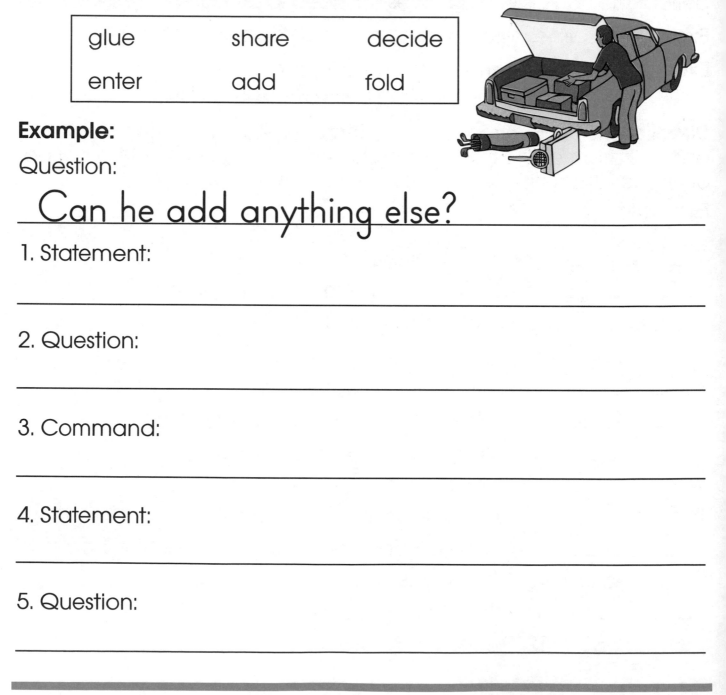

Example:

Question:

Can he add anything else?

1. Statement:

_____

2. Question:

_____

3. Command:

_____

4. Statement:

_____

5. Question:

_____

Name: _____

Kinds of Sentences

Directions: Use the group of words below to write three sentences: a **statement**, a **question** and a **command**.

add	can	these	he	quickly	numbers

Example:

Statement:

He can add these numbers quickly.

Question:

Can he can add these numbers quickly?

Command:

Add these numbers quickly.

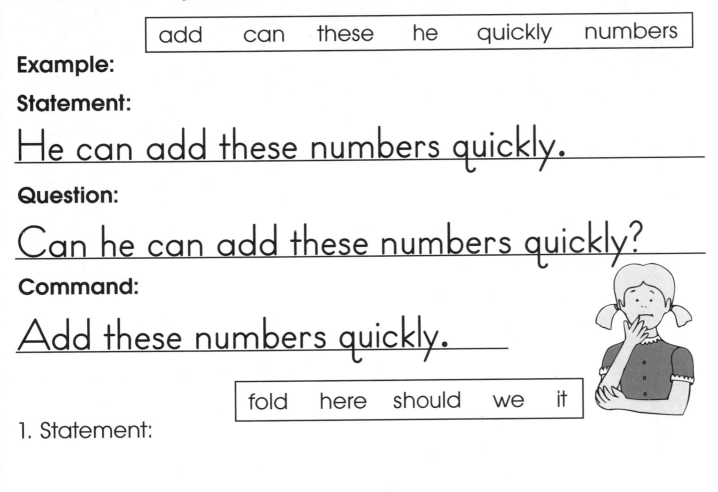

fold	here	should	we	it

1. Statement:

_____

2. Question:

_____

3. Command:

_____

Name: _____

Vocabulary: Completing a Story

Directions: Use verbs to complete the story below. The verbs that tell about things that happened in the past will end in **ed**.

Last week, Amy and I _____

a contest. We were supposed to make a

card to give to a child in a hospital. First, we

_____ a big sheet of white paper

in half to make the card. Then we _____ to draw a

rainbow on the front. Amy started coloring the rainbow all by herself.

"Wait!" I said. "We both _____ the contest. Let me help!"

"Okay," Amy said. "Let's _____ . You _____

a color, and then I'll _____ a color." It was more fun

when we _____ . When we finished making the rainbow,

we _____ to _____ a sun to the picture. I cut

one out of yellow paper. Then Amy _____ it just above

the rainbow. Well, our card didn't win the contest, but it did make

a little boy with a broken leg smile. Amy and I felt so happy! We

_____ to go right home and make some more cards!

Name: _____

Review

Directions: Write directions to go with each picture. Remember that a direction is a command and begins with a verb.

How To Make a Sky at Night

1. _____

2. _____

3. _____

How To Paint a Wagon Orange

1. _____

2. _____

3. _____

© 1999 American Education Publishing Co.

Name: _____

Homophones

Homophones are words that sound the same but are spelled differently and have different meanings.

Directions: Use the homophones in the box to answer the riddles below.

main	meat	peace	dear	to
mane	meet	piece	deer	too

1. Which word has the word **pie** in it? _____

2. Which word rhymes with **ear** and is an animal? _____

3. Which word rhymes with **shoe** and means **also**? _____

4. Which word has the word **eat** in it and is something you might eat? _____

5. Which word has the same letters as the word **read** but in a different order? _____

6. Which word rhymes with **train** and is something on a pony? _____

7. Which word, if it began with a capital letter, might be the name of an important street? _____

8. Which word sounds like a number but has only two letters? _____

9. Which word rhymes with and is a synonym for **greet**? _____

10. Which word rhymes with the last syllable in **police** and can mean quiet? _____

Homophones

Directions: Cut out each honeybee at the bottom of the page and glue it on the flower with its homophone.

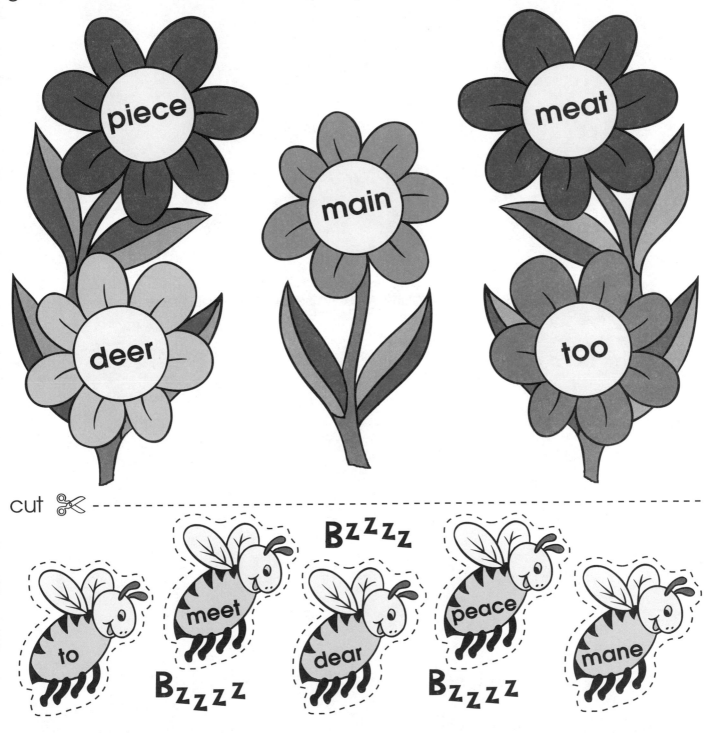

cut ✂ -

Page is blank for cutting exercise on previous page.

Name: _____

Homophones: Sentences

Directions: Write a word from the box to complete each sentence.

main	meat	peace	dear	two
mane	meet	piece	deer	too

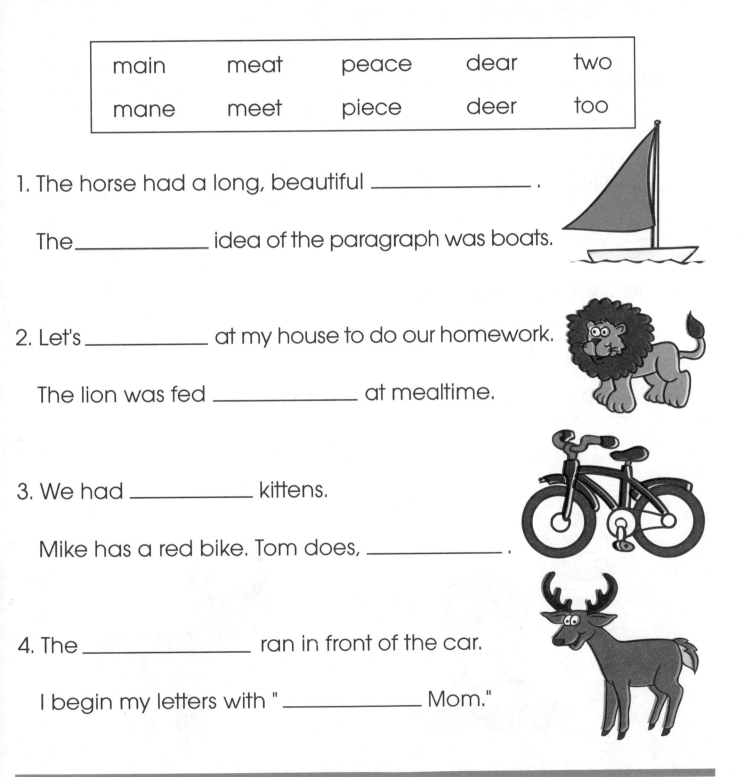

1. The horse had a long, beautiful _____ .

   The _____ idea of the paragraph was boats.

2. Let's _____ at my house to do our homework.

   The lion was fed _____ at mealtime.

3. We had _____ kittens.

   Mike has a red bike. Tom does, _____ .

4. The _____ ran in front of the car.

   I begin my letters with " _____ Mom."

Homophones: Spelling

Directions: Circle the word in each sentence which is not spelled correctly. Then write the word correctly.

1. Please meat me at the park. _____

2. I would like a peace of pie. _____

3. There were too cookies left. _____

4. The horse's main needed to be brushed. _____

5. We saw a dear in the forest. _____

Name: _____

SPELLING 3

Homophones: Rhymes

Directions: Use homophones to create two-lined rhymes.

Example: I found it a **pain**

To comb the horse's **mane**!

1. _____

_____

2. _____

_____

3. _____

_____

41

© 1999 American Education Publishing Co.

Review

Directions: Write two statements about the picture, one command and one question.

Statements:

1. _____

2. _____

Question:

_____

Command:

_____

Name: _____

Short Vowels

Short vowel patterns usually have a single vowel followed by a consonant sound.

Short a is the sound you hear in the word **can**.
Short e is the sound you hear in the word **men**.
Short i is the sound you hear in the word **pig**.
Short o is the sound you hear in the word **pot**.
Short u is the sound you hear in the word **truck**.

fast	stop
spin	track
wish	lunch
bread	block

Directions: Use the words in the box to answer the questions below.

Which word:

begins with the same sound as **blast** and ends with the same sound as **look**? _____

rhymes with **stack**? _____

begins with the same sound as **phone** and ends with the same sound as **lost**? _____

has the same vowel sound as **hen**? _____

rhymes with **crunch**? _____

begins with the same sound as **spot** and ends with the same sound as **can**? _____

begins with the same sound as **win** and ends with the same sound as **crush**? _____

has the word **top** in it? _____

Name: _____

Short Vowels: Sentences

Directions: Use the words in the box to complete each sentence.

fast	wish	truck	bread	sun
best	stop	track	lunch	block

Race cars can go very_____ .

Carol packs a _____ for Ted before school.

Throw a penny in the well and make a _____ .

The _____ had a flat tire.

My favorite kind of _____ is whole wheat.

Short Vowels: Spelling

Directions: Circle the word in each sentence which is not spelled correctly. Then write the word correctly.

1. Be sure to stopp at the red light. _____

2. The train goes down the trak. _____

3. Please put the bred in the toaster. _____

4. I need another blok to finish. _____

5. The beasst player won a trophy. _____

6. Blow out the candles and
   make a wiish. _____

7. The truk blew its horn. _____

Review

Directions: Write one sentence about each picture. Be sure to begin each sentence with a capital letter and end it with a period.

_____

_____

_____

_____

Name: _____

Long Vowels

Long vowels are the letters **a, e, i, o** and **u** which say the letter name sound.

Long a is the sound you hear in **cane**.

Long e is the sound you hear in **green**.

Long i is the sound you hear in **pie**.

Long o is the sound you hear in **bowl**.

Long u is the sound you hear in **cube**.

lame	goal
pain	few
street	fright
nose	gray
bike	fuse

Directions: Use the words in the box to answer the questions below.

1. Add one letter to each of these words to make words from the box.

   ray _____ use _____ right _____

2. Change one letter from each word to make a word from the box.

   pail _____ goat _____

   late _____ bite _____

3. Write the word from the box that . . .

   has the long **e** sound. _____

   rhymes with **you**. _____

   is a homophone for **knows**. _____

Name: _____

Long Vowels: Sentences

Directions: Use the words in the box to complete each sentence.

lame	goal	pain	few	bike
street	fright	nose	gray	fuse

1. Look both ways before crossing the _____ .

2. My _____ had a flat tire.

3. Our walk through the haunted house

   gave us such a _____ .

4. I kicked the soccer ball and scored a _____ .

5. The _____ clouds mean rain is coming.

6. Cover your _____ when you sneeze.

7. We blew a _____ at my house last night.

Name: _____

Long Vowels

Directions: Use long vowel words from the box to answer the clues below. Write the letters of the words on the lines.

| few | bike | dime | goal | fuse | lame | street | nose | fright | pain |

1. ___ ___ ___ ___ ___ [ ] (rhymes with **night**)

2. ___ ___ [ ] ___ ___ ___ (could be Main or Maple)

3. ___ [ ] ___ (synonym for **a couple**)

4. ___ ___ [ ] ___ (rhymes with **tame**)

5. ___ ___ ___ [ ] (can be ridden on a trail)

6. ___ ___ ___ [ ] (homophone for **pane**)

7. [ ] ___ ___ ___ (ten of these make a dollar)

8. ___ [ ] ___ ___ (changing one letter of this word makes **goat**)

9. ___ [ ] ___ ___ (has the word **use** in it)

10. ___ ___ [ ] ___ (homophone for **knows**)

Now, read the letters in the boxes from top to bottom to find out what kind of a job you did!

Review

Directions: Imagine that you are a puppy outside. What would you do and see? Write sentences below to tell what you would do and see.

_____

_____

_____

_____

_____

_____

_____

Name: _____

Adjectives

Directions: Use the words in the box to answer the questions below.
Use each word only once.

polite	careless	neat	shy	selfish	thoughtful

1. Someone who is quiet and needs
   some time to make new friends is _____ .

2. A person who says "please"
   and "thank you" is _____ .

3. Someone who always
   puts all the toys away is _____ .

4. A person who won't share with
   others is being _____ .

5. A person who leaves a bike out
   all night is being _____ .

6. Someone who thinks of others is _____ .

Name: _____

Adjectives

Directions: Use the adjectives in the box to answer the questions below.

polite	careless	neat	shy	selfish	thoughtful

1. Change a letter in each word to make an adjective.

     near   _____

     why   _____

2. Write the word that rhymes with each of these.

     fell dish   _____

     not full   _____

     hair mess _____

3. Find these words in the adjectives. Write the adjective.

     at   _____

     are   _____

     it   _____

Name: _____

Adjectives: Spelling

Directions: Circle the word in each sentence which is not spelled correctly. Then write the word correctly.

1. John isn't shelfish at all. _____

2. He sharred his lunch with me today. _____

3. I was careles and forgot to bring mine. _____

4. My father says if I planed better,
   that wouldn't happen all the time. _____

5. John is kind of quiet, and I used
   to think he was shie. _____

6. Now, I know he is really thotful. _____

7. He's also very polyte and always
   asks before he borrows anything. _____

8. He would never just reach over
   and grabb something he wanted. _____

9. I'm glad John desided to be my friend. _____

Adjectives: Explaining Sentences

Directions: Use a word from the box to tell about a person in each picture below. Then write a sentence that explains why you chose that word.

| polite   neat   careless   shy   selfish   thoughtful |

The word I picked: _____

I think so because . . .

_____

The word I picked: _____

I think so because . . .

_____

The word I picked: _____

I think so because . . .

_____

Name: _____

Adjectives

Directions: Look at each picture. Then add adjectives to the sentences. Use colors, numbers, words from the box and any other words you need to describe each picture.

Example:

polite	neat	careless
shy	selfish	thoughtful

The boy shared his pencil.

The polite boy shared his red pencil.

The girl dropped her coat.

_____

The boy played with cars.

_____

The boy put books away.

_____

Name: _____

Adjectives: Create a Word Puzzle

Directions: Make your own word puzzle! Write the words from the box in the puzzle below. Write some words across and others from top to bottom. Make some words cross each other. Fill the extra squares with other letters. See if someone else can find the words from the box in your puzzle!

| polite | careless | neat | shy | selfish | thoughtful |

Your puzzle will look like the one below. It has two of the words in it. Can you find them?

l	a	e	n	x	f	y	h
c	a	r	e	l	e	s	s
y	u	a	a	r	n	m	z
g	w	i	t	b	i	v	s

Now, make your own puzzle!

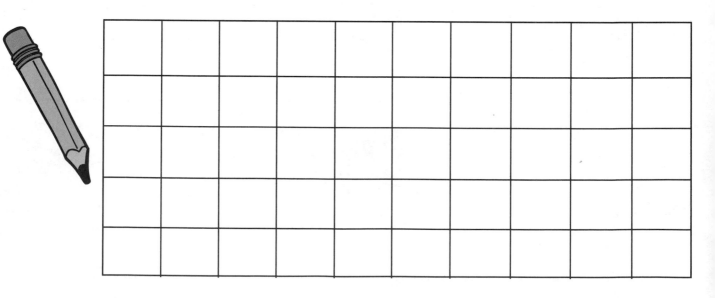

Name: _____

Review

Directions: Complete the stories below using your own ideas. Use adjectives to make some of your sentences longer.

One day, a very thoughtful girl came to the park where I was playing with my friends. She was carrying a big box.

_____

_____

_____

My friend Jamie used to be very shy. He never said anything in class. Then one day something happened to change that.

_____

_____

_____

57

C, K, CK Words: Spelling

Directions: Write the words from the box that answer the questions.

| crowd | keeper | cost | pack | kangaroo | thick |

1. Which words spell the **k** sound with a **k**?

_____

2. Which words spell the **k** sound with a **c**?

_____

3. Which words spell the **k** sound with **ck**?

_____

4. Circle the letters that spell **k** in these words:

cook   black   cool   kite

cake   pocket   poke

5. Which words from the box rhyme with each of these?

tossed _____   deeper _____

proud _____   all in blue _____

Name: _____

C, K, CK Words: Sentences

The **k** sound can be spelled with a **c**, **k** or **ck** after a short vowel sound.

Directions: Use the words from the box to complete the sentences. Use each word only once.

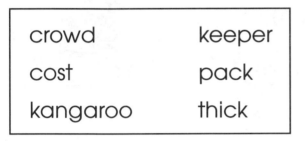

crowd	keeper
cost	pack
kangaroo	thick

1. On sunny days, there is always a _____ of people at the zoo.

2. It doesn't _____ much to get into the zoo.

3. We always get hungry, so we _____ a picnic lunch.

4. We like to watch the _____ .

5. Its _____ tail helps it jump and walk.

6. The_____ always makes sure the cages are clean.

C, K, CK Words: Sentences

Remember: every sentence must have a noun that tells who or what is doing something and a verb that tells what the noun is doing.

Directions: Parts of each sentence below are missing. Rewrite each sentence, adding a noun or a verb, periods and capital letters.

Example:

read a book every day (needs a noun)

Leon reads a book every day. _____

1. packed a lunch

_____

2. the crowd at the beach

_____

3. cost too much

_____

4. kangaroos and their babies

_____

5. was too thick to chew

_____

Name: _____

C, K, CK Words: Joining Sentences

Joining words are words that make two sentences into one longer sentence. Here are some words that join sentences:

and — if both sentences are about the same noun or verb.

> **Example:** Tom is in my class at school, **and** he lives near me.

but — if the second sentence says something different from the first sentence.

> **Example:** Julie walks to school with me, **but** today she is sick.

or — if each sentence names a different thing you could do.

> **Example:** We could go to my house, **or** we could go to yours.

Directions: Join each set of sentences below using the words **and**, **but** or **or**.

1. Those socks usually cost a lot. This pack of ten socks is cheaper.

_____

_____

2. The kangaroo has a pouch. It lives in Australia.

_____

_____

3. The zoo keeper can start to work early. She can stay late.

_____

_____

C, K, CK Words: Joining Sentences

If and **when** can be joining words, too.

Directions: Read each set of sentences. Then join the two sentences to make one longer sentence.

Example: The apples will need to be washed.
The apples are dirty.

The apples will need to be washed if they are dirty.

1. The size of the crowd grew. It grew when the game began.

_____

_____

2. Be careful driving in the fog. The fog is thick.

_____

_____

3. Pack your suitcases. Do it when you wake up in the morning.

_____

_____

C, K, CK Words: Joining Sentences

Other words that can join sentences are:

when — **When** we got there, the show had already started.

after — **After** I finished my homework, I watched TV.

because — You can't go by yourself, **because** you are too young.

Directions: Use the joining words to make the two short sentences into one longer one.

1. **when** The keeper opened the door. The bear got out.

_____

_____

2. **because** I didn't buy the tickets. They cost too much.

_____

_____

3. **after** The kangaroo ate lunch. He took a nap.

_____

_____

4. **when** The door opened. The crowd rushed in.

_____

_____

5. **after** I cut the bread. Everyone had a slice.

_____

_____

C, K, CK Words: Joining Sentences

Directions: Use **because**, **after** or **when** to join each set of sentences into one longer sentence.

1. I pack my own lunch. I always put in some fruit.

_____

_____

2. I would like to be a zoo keeper. I love animals.

_____

_____

3. I was surprised there was such a crowd. It cost a lot.

_____

_____

4. I beat the eggs for two minutes. They were thick and yellow.

_____

_____

Name: _____

C, K, CK Words: Crossword Puzzle

Directions: Write the word that completes each sentence by the correct number in the puzzle.

Across:
2. A lot of people make a ____.
3. This glue is too stiff and ____.
6. The ____ is from Australia.

Down:
1. Cars ____ a lot of money.
4. The ____ takes care of zoo animals.
5. Every morning, I ____ my lunch.

C, K, CK Words: Completing a Story

Directions: Use **c**, **k**, or **ck** words to complete this story. Some of the verbs are past tense and need to end with **ed**.

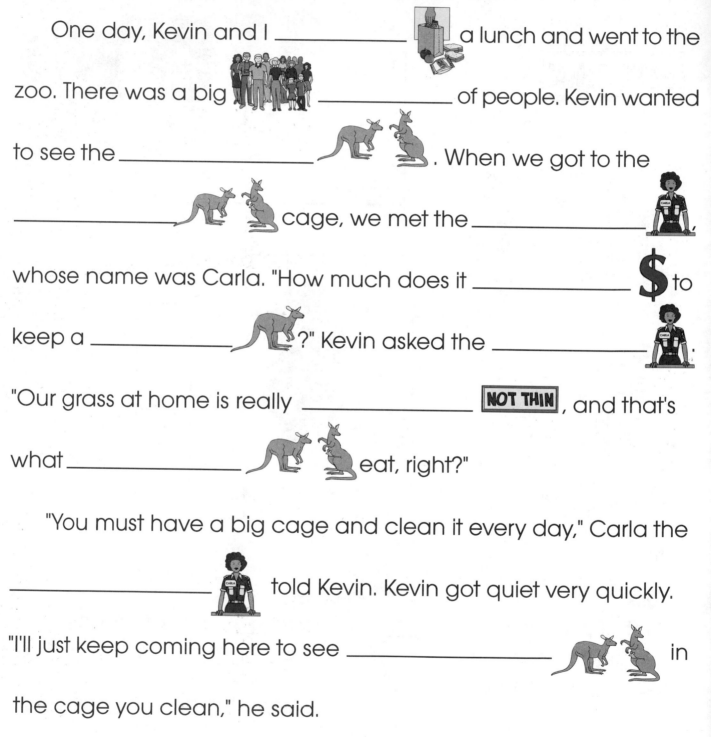

One day, Kevin and I _____ a lunch and went to the

zoo. There was a big _____ of people. Kevin wanted

to see the _____ . When we got to the

_____ cage, we met the _____

whose name was Carla. "How much does it _____ $ to

keep a _____ ?" Kevin asked the _____ .

"Our grass at home is really _____ NOT THIN , and that's

what _____ eat, right?"

"You must have a big cage and clean it every day," Carla the

_____ told Kevin. Kevin got quiet very quickly.

"I'll just keep coming here to see _____ in

the cage you clean," he said.

66

Name: _____

Review

Directions: Write a TV commercial for a zoo.

1. First, write all your ideas on another sheet of paper. Think: Why should people come to the zoo? What would they see there? What would be fun?
2. Then put your ideas in order. You might decide not to use some of them.
3. Write your commercial in complete sentences in the space below.
4. Pretend you are on television and read your commercial to someone.

_____

_____

_____

_____

_____

_____

_____

S Words: Spelling

The **s** sound can be spelled with an **s**, **ss**, **c** or **ce**.

Directions: Use the words from the box to complete the sentences below. Write each word only once.

center	pencil	space
address	police	darkness

1. I drew a circle in the _____ of the page.

2. I'll write to you if you tell me your _____ .

3. She pushed too hard and broke the point on her _____ .

4. If you hear a noise at night, call the _____ .

5. It was night, and I couldn't see him in the _____ .

6. There's not enough _____ for me to sit next to you.

Name: _____

S Words: Spelling

Directions: Write the words from the box that answer the questions.

| center | pencil | space | address | police | darkness |

1. Which words spell the **s** sound with **ss**?

_____

2. Which words spell **s** with a **c**?

_____

3. Which words spell **s** with **ce**?

_____

4. Write two other words you know that spell **s** with an **s**.

_____

5. Circle the letters that spell **s** in these words.

decide   kiss   careless   ice

cost   fierce   sentence

6. Put these letters in order to make words from the box.

sdsdera _____   sdserakn _____

clipoe _____   clipne _____

capse _____   retnce _____

Name: _____

S Words: Sentences

Directions: Write your own sentences using the word pairs below.

Example: class   share

In my class at school, we all

share the work.

1. decide   center

_____

_____

2. space   address

_____

_____

3. darkness   police

_____

_____

Name: _____

C and S Words: Spelling

The letter **c** can make the **k** sound or the **s** sound.

Example: **c**ount, **c**ity

Directions: Write **k** or **s** to show how the **c** in each word sounds.

cave	_____	copy	_____	force	_____
become	_____	dance	_____	city	_____
certain	_____	contest	_____	cool	_____

Directions: Use the words from the box to answer these questions.

center	pencil	space	address	police	darkness

1. Which word begins with the same sound as **simple** and ends with the same sound as **fur**? _____

2. Which word begins with the same sound as **average** and ends with the same sound as **circus**? _____

3. Which word begins with the same sound as **popcorn** and ends with the same sound as **glass**? _____

4. Which word begins and ends with the same sound as **pool**?

_____

5. Which word begins with the same sound as **city** and ends with the same sound as **kiss**? _____

6. Which word begins and ends with the same sound as **delicious**?

_____

Name: _____

Two Kinds of Writing

Some writing tells how someone looks. Other writing tells a story. It tells what someone has done and why he or she did that.

Directions: Read the sentences about the girl. Then write the same kinds of sentences about the boy.

Example:

Tell how she looks:

She looks tired and wet.
Her shoes are full of rain.

Tell a story about her:

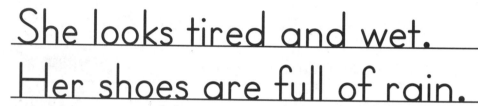
She didn't get up in time.
She missed her bus.

Tell how he looks:

_____

_____

Tell a story about him:

_____

_____

Name: _____

C and S Words: Spelling

Directions: Circle the words which are not spelled correctly in the story. Then write each word correctly on the lines below.

One day, Peter and I were sitting on a bench at the park. A polise woman came and sat in the empty spase beside us. "Have you seen a little dog with thik black fur?" she asked. She was very poolite. "Remember that dog?" I asked Peter. "He was just here!" Peter nodded. He was too shie to say anything.

"Give us his adress," I said. "We'll find him and take him home." She got out a pensil and wrote the addres in the senter of a piece of paper. Peter and I desided to walk down the street the way the dog had gone. There was a krowd of people at a cherch we passed, but no dog.

Then it started getting late. "We better go home," Peter said. "I can't see in this drakness, anyway."

As we turned around to go back, there was the little dog! He had been following us! We took him to the adress. The girl who came to the door grabed him and huged him tight. "I'm sorry I let you wander away," she told the dog. "I'll never be so carless again." I thought she was going to kis us, too. We left just in time!

_____   _____   _____

_____   _____   _____

_____   _____   _____

_____   _____   _____

_____   _____   _____

Name: _____

Review

Directions:

1. Look at the pictures and make up a story.
2. Write the story in sentences on another sheet of paper. Do your sentences tell what happened in the order it happened? Does each sentence have a noun and a verb? Did you combine some short sentences with **or, and, but, because, when** or **after**?
3. Read your story to someone. Are there any changes that would make your story clearer?
4. Copy your story in the space under the pictures.
5. Then read your story to someone else.

_____

_____

_____

_____

_____

_____

_____

Name: _____

Suffixes

A **suffix** is a word part added to the end of a word. Suffixes add to or change the meaning of the word.

Example: sad + ly = sadly

Below are some suffixes and their meanings.

ment	state of being, quality of, act of
ly	like or in a certain way
ness	state of being
ful	full of
less	without

Directions: The words in the box have suffixes. Use the suffix meanings above to match each word with its meaning below. Write the words on the lines.

friendly	cheerful	safely	sleeveless	speechless
kindness	amazement	sickness	peaceful	excitement

1. in a safe way   __ __ __ __ __ __
                        6

2. full of cheer   __ __ __ __ __ __ __ __
                              2

3. full of peace   __ __ __ __ __ __ __
                     4

4. state of being amazed   __ __ __ __ __ __ __ __ __
                                        5

5. state of being excited   __ __ __ __ __ __ __ __ __
                              1

6. without speech   __ __ __ __ __ __ __ __ __ __
                                   3

Use the numbered letters to find the missing word below.

You are now on your way to becoming a

__ __ __ __ __ __   of suffixes!
5   6   3   1   4   2

Suffixes: Adverbs

Adverbs are words that describe verbs. Adverbs tell where, when or how. Most adverbs end in the suffix **ly**.

Directions: Complete each sentence with the correct part of speech.

Example:

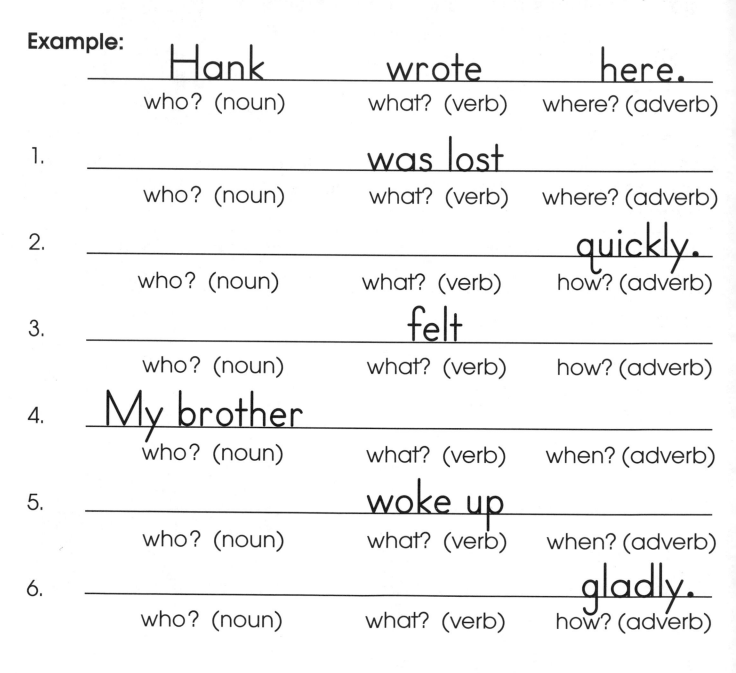

Hank wrote here.
who? (noun)　　what? (verb)　　where? (adverb)

1. _____ **was lost** _____
who? (noun)　　what? (verb)　　where? (adverb)

2. _____ _____ **quickly.**
who? (noun)　　what? (verb)　　how? (adverb)

3. _____ **felt** _____
who? (noun)　　what? (verb)　　how? (adverb)

4. **My brother** _____ _____
who? (noun)　　what? (verb)　　when? (adverb)

5. _____ **woke up** _____
who? (noun)　　what? (verb)　　when? (adverb)

6. _____ _____ **gladly.**
who? (noun)　　what? (verb)　　how? (adverb)

Name: _____

Suffixes: Root Words

A **root word** is a word before a suffix is added.

Example: In the word **hope**ful, the root word is **hope**.

DON'T BE CLUELESS!

Directions: Each egg contains a root word. Cut out each egg and match it with a basket so that it forms a new word. Write the new word on the lines on the basket.

baskets labeled: ly, ment, ness, ful, less

I CAN'T STAND THE EGGCITEMENT!

cut ✂ -

eggs: friend, cheer, safe, sleeve, speech, kind, amaze, sick, peace

Page is blank for cutting exercise on previous page.

Name: _____

Suffixes: Sentences

Directions: Use a word from the box to complete each sentence.

cheerful	softness	encouragement
kindness	safely	friendly

1. The _____ dog licked me and wagged his tail.

2. Jeff is happy and _____ .

3. To ride your bike _____ , you should wear a helmet.

4. My aunt is known for her thoughtfulness and _____ .

5. I love the _____ of my cat's fur.

6. The teacher gave her class a lot of _____ .

79

© 1999 American Education Publishing Co.

Review

Directions: Pretend you are in charge of creating rules for your family or class at school. Write five rules you would make. Try to use words with suffixes.

Kindness

Safely

1. _____

2. _____

3. _____

4. _____

5. _____

Name: _____

Prefixes

Prefixes are word parts added to the beginning of a root word. Prefixes add to or change the meaning of the word.

Example: **re**make — to make something again.

re — again   un — not   dis — not or reverse   in — in or not

Directions: Read the meanings on each treasure chest lid. Then glue the correct word onto each treasure chest.

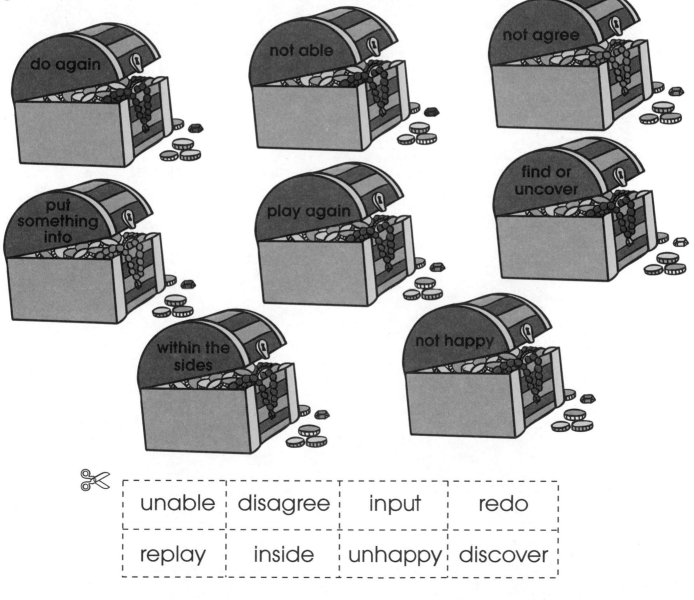

do again   not able   not agree

put something into   play again   find or uncover

within the sides   not happy

| unable | disagree | input | redo |
| replay | inside | unhappy | discover |

---

81   © 1999 American Education Publishing Co.

Page is blank for cutting exercise on previous page.

Name: _____

Prefixes: Sentences

Directions: Match each sentence with the word which completes it. Then write the word on the line.

1. The farmer was _____ because it • didn't rain.

• input

2. The scientist tried to _____ the • secret formula.

• redo

3. The child _____ his report • into the computer.

• unhappy

4. We were _____ to do the • work without help.

• disagree

5. My brother and I _____ about • which show to watch.

• replay

6. The umpire called for a _____ of • the game.

• discover

7. We had to stay _____ when • it got cold.

• inside

8. I spilled my milk on my paper and had to • _____ my homework.

• unable

Name: _____

Prefixes

Directions: Create new words by combining prefixes and root words. Write at least three new words for each prefix. You may also add some of your own root words.

Root Words			
to	door	field	honest
approve	appear	move	write
enter	cover	afraid	bend
call	continue	even	

Prefixes

un	in
re	**dis**

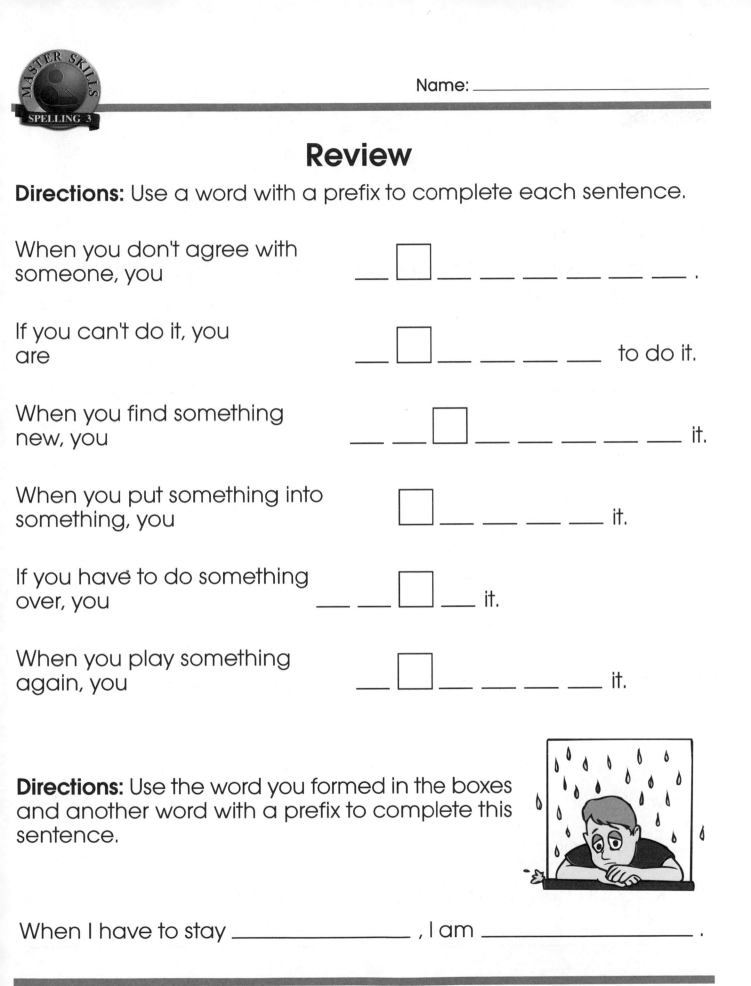

Name: _____

Review

Directions: Use a word with a prefix to complete each sentence.

When you don't agree with
someone, you   __ □ __ __ __ __ __ __ .

If you can't do it, you
are   __ □ __ __ __ __ to do it.

When you find something
new, you   __ __ □ __ __ __ __ __ __ it.

When you put something into
something, you   □ __ __ __ __ it.

If you have to do something
over, you   __ __ □ __ it.

When you play something
again, you   __ □ __ __ __ __ it.

Directions: Use the word you formed in the boxes and another word with a prefix to complete this sentence.

When I have to stay _____ , I am _____ .

Name: _____

Synonyms

Synonyms are words which mean almost the same thing.

Example: sick — ill

Directions: Use words from the box to help you complete the sentences below.

glad	fast	noisy	filthy	angry

1. When I am mad, I could also say I am _____ .

2. To be _____ is the same as being happy.

3. After playing outside, I thought I was dirty, but Mom said I was _____ !

4. I tried not to be too loud, but I couldn't help being a little _____ .

5. If you're too _____ , or speedy, you may not do a careful job.

Think of another pair of synonyms. Write them on the lines.

_____   _____

Synonyms

Directions: Cut out the sails below. Glue each one to the boat whose synonym matches it.

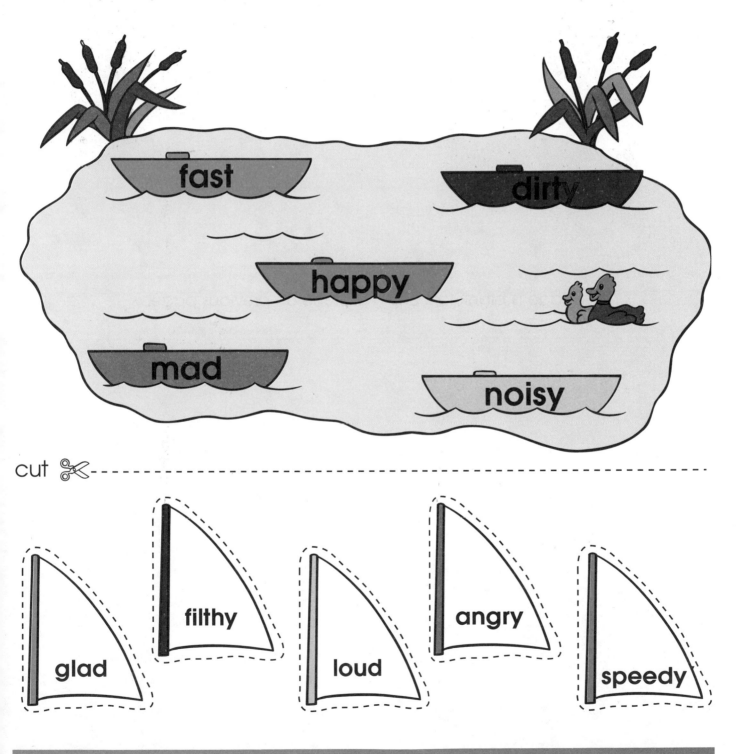

cut ✂ -

glad

filthy

loud

angry

speedy

Page is blank for cutting exercise on previous page.

Name: _____

Antonyms

Antonyms are words that have opposite meanings.

Example: neat — sloppy

Directions: Cut out each frog below and glue it to the lily pad with its antonym.

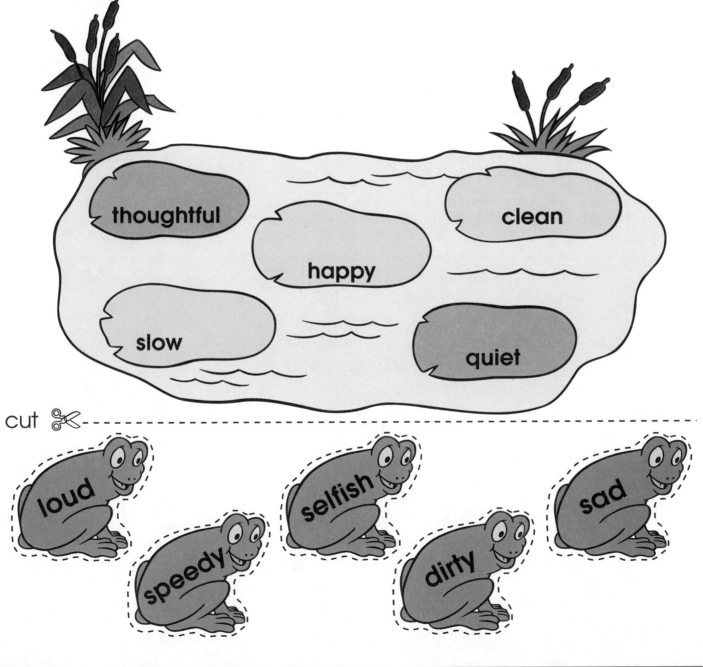

cut ✂ -

Page is blank for cutting exercise on previous page.

Antonyms

Directions: Use antonyms from the box to complete the sentences below.

speedy	clean	quiet	thoughtful	happy

1. If we get too loud, the teacher will ask us to get _____ .

2. She was sad to lose her puppy, but she was _____

   to find it again.

3. Mark got dirty, so he had to scrub himself _____ .

4. Janna was too _____ when

   she did her homework, so she tried

   to be slow when she did it over.

5. Dave was too selfish to share his cookies,

   but Deborah was _____ enough to share hers.

Think of another pair of antonyms. Write them on the lines.

_____   _____

Name: _____

Contractions

A **contraction** is a short way to write two words together. Some letters are left out, but an apostrophe takes their place.

Directions: Write the words from the box that answer the questions.

| hasn't | you've | aren't | we've | weren't |

1. Write the correct contractions below.

   Example:

   I have   _____ I've _____   was not   _____ wasn't

   we have _____   you have _____

   are not _____   were not _____

   has not _____

2. Write two words from the box that are contractions using **have**.

_____   _____

3. Write three words from the box that are contractions using **not**.

_____ _____ _____

Contractions

Directions: In each sentence below, underline the two words that could be made into a contraction. Write the contraction on the line. Use each contraction from the box only once.

Example: The boys <u>have not</u> gone camping in a long time.

haven't

hasn't	you've	aren't
we've	weren't	

1. After a while, we were not sure it was the right direction. _____

2. I think we have been this way before. _____

3. We have been waiting, but our guide has not come yet. _____

4. Did you say you have been here with your sister? _____

5. You are not going to give up and go back, are you? _____

Name: _____

Contractions: Spelling

Directions: Circle the two words in each sentence that are not spelled correctly. Then write the words correctly.

1. Arn't you going to shere your cookie with me?

_____   _____

2. We planed a long time, but we still wern't ready.

_____   _____

3. My pensil hassn't broken yet today.

_____   _____

4. We arn't going because we don't have the correct adress.

_____   _____

5. Youve stired the soup too much.

_____   _____

6. Weave tried to be as neet as possible.

_____   _____

7. She hasnt seen us in this darknes.

_____   _____

Name: _____

Silly Sentence Book

Directions: Make several copies of the sentence pattern below and on page 97. Then write words in each box and draw a picture to illustrate them. Cut out each pattern. Staple them all together at the top. Cut apart each box on the cutting lines. Then flip the three boxes to read silly sentences.

Example: The brown bear rode its one-wheeled bike to the store.

Noun	Verb	Location
The brown bear	rode its one-wheeled bike	to the store.

Silly Sentence Pattern

Noun	Verb	Location

© 1999 American Education Publishing Co.

Page is blank for cutting exercise on previous page.

Silly Sentence Book

Noun	Verb	Location

Noun	Verb	Location

Page is blank for cutting exercise on previous page.

Name: _____

Alphabetical Order

Alphabetical order is the order in which letters come in the alphabet.

Directions: Write the words in alphabetical order. If the first letter is the same, use the second letter of each word to decide which word comes first. If the second letter is also the same, look at the third letter of each word to decide.

Example: w(i)sh   w(a)sp   w(o)n't

1. w**a**sp
2. w**i**sh
3. w**o**n't

bench   flag   bowl

1. _____

2. _____

3. _____

egg   nod   neat

1. _____

2. _____

3. _____

dog   dart   drag

1. _____

2. _____

3. _____

skipped   stairs   stones

1. _____

2. _____

3. _____

Name: _____

Dictionary Skills

A **dictionary** is a book that tells how to pronounce and spell words and what words mean.

The words in a dictionary are in alphabetical order. That makes them easy to find. To look up a word, use the guide words. **Guide words** are at the top of each page. The word on the left is the first word listed on the page. The word on the right is the last word listed on the page.

Directions: Answer the questions about this dictionary page.

aardvark	**atlas**
aardvark — an animal that is much like an anteater	**apple** — a fruit
all — every one of something	**ark** — a large boat
ant — a small insect	**atlas** — a book of maps

1. What are the guide words on this page? _____

2. What is an animal that is like an anteater? _____

3. What is a type of boat? _____

4. What is an atlas? _____

5. Which word is a kind of fruit? _____

6. What is the last word on this dictionary page? _____

Dictionary Skills

Directions: Cross out the words in the box that would not belong on this page. Then write the rest of the words in alphabetical order on the blanks below.

octopus   **quilt**

_____   _____

_____   _____

_____   _____

_____   _____

_____   _____

octopus	water	old	part
stairs	order	frog	quarrel
pink	paint	orange	poor
porch	oats	quilt	open

Name: _____

Paragraphs

A **paragraph** is a group of sentences that all tell about the same thing.

Directions: In each paragraph below, draw a line through the sentence that doesn't belong. Circle all the contractions.

We have a rule at our house. After you've done your homework, you can watch one TV show. I walk home from school. Tonight I don't have any homework, so I guess I can't watch TV.

In our class, we aren't allowed to chew gum. The teacher says he can tell when we've got gum in our mouths. He says it makes us look like cows. That hasn't stopped Jimmy, though. He likes ice cream better. He chews gum when the teacher isn't looking.

My sister and I weren't supposed to cut through the field on the way home from school today. My friend Carla rides the bus home. Now, I know why Mom told us not to do that. The field is full of mud—and so are our shoes!

We've got a dog named Pepper at our house. I feed Pepper every day, but my brother hasn't helped in a long time. He's taller than I am. I think Pepper likes me better than he likes my brother!

Name: _____

Paragraphs: Sentences in Order

Directions: Read the sentences below. Write numbers to show the correct order for the sentences in a paragraph.

_____ Sally picked out a cute stray puppy with black feet.

_____ Then they went to a place that takes care of stray animals.

_____ One day, Sally's parents told her she could have a puppy.

_____ When he was all cleaned up, his feet weren't black anymore!

_____ The puppies at the pet store cost too much.

_____ First, they went to buy a puppy at a pet store.

_____ Sally and her parents took him home and gave him a bath.

_____ The wind was blowing, and the snow was very deep.

_____ In his dream, he was at the North Pole.

_____ One night, Mike couldn't go to sleep.

_____ Then his brother woke him up.

_____ "Mike!" his brother yelled. "You've left the window open, and it's freezing in here!"

_____ When he finally fell asleep, he had a strange dream.

© 1999 American Education Publishing Co.

Review

Directions: Follow the steps below to write a paragraph about this picture. Your paragraph could tell what you see in the picture or you could make up a story about what is happening here.

1. First, write all your ideas on another sheet of paper.

2. Choose the ideas you want to use in your paragraph. Leave out the ones that don't belong.

3. Put your ideas in order so they make sense.

4. Write them in sentences on another sheet of paper.

5. Read your sentences to someone and ask if you need to make any changes.

6. After you make the changes, write your paragraph below.

_____

_____

_____

_____

_____

_____

Research Project

Directions: Choose any animal that interests you. What kinds of things do you already know about this animal? What do you want to find out about it?

This research project will help you organize the facts you find and use them to write a paragraph.

First, find information about your animal. Use an encyclopedia, a special book about the animal or the Internet. Write your facts here.

Example:

Animal: __the tuatara, a lizard–like creature__

Where does it live? __lives only on small, chilly islands off New Zealand__

Animal: _____

Where does it live? _____

What does it eat and how does it catch or eat its food?

_____

Describe in detail what it looks like. _____

_____

_____

Other interesting facts: _____

_____

© 1999 American Education Publishing Co.

Research Project

Use the facts you researched to write sentences for a paragraph. Indent the first word.

Sample first sentence:

The tuatara is an interesting lizard–like creature.

_____

_____

_____

_____

_____

_____

_____

_____

Now, have an adult help you look over your paragraph. Correct any mistakes, such as spelling, capital letters and periods. Then make a final copy of your paragraph in your best handwriting.

Glossary

Adjectives: Words that describe nouns. Examples: **tall, four, cold, happy**.

Adverbs: Words that describe verbs. They often tell how, when or where. Examples: **here, today, quickly**.

Antonyms: Words that are opposites. Example: **hot** and **cold**.

Commands: Sentences that tell someone to do something. They usually begin with a verb or the word **please**.

Consonants: All the letters except **a, e, i, o** and **u**.

Contractions: Words that are a short way to write two words together. Example: **isn't** means **is not**.

Directions: Sentences that are written as commands, telling someone to do something.

Guide Words: Words at the top of a dictionary page. They are the first and last words on that page.

Homophones: Words that sound the same but are spelled differently and have different meanings.

Joining Words: Words that combine ideas in a sentence, such as **and, but, or, because**.

Long Vowels: The letters **a, e, i, o** and **u** which say the "long" or letter name sound. **Long a** is the sound you hear in **hay**. **Long e** is the sound you hear in **me**. **Long i** is the sound you hear in **pie**. **Long o** is the sound you hear in **no**. **Long u** is the sound you hear in **cute**.

Nouns: Words that name a person, place or thing.

Opposites: Words that are different in every way. Example: **black** and **white**.

Paragraphs: Groups of sentences that tell about the same thing.

Past Tense: Form of verbs that means that it has already happened.

Plural: A noun that refers to more than one thing.

Prefixes: Word parts added to the beginning of a word to change or add to its meaning. Example: **re**do.

Present Tense: Form of verbs that means that something is happening right now.

Questions: Asking sentences. A question begins with a capital letter and ends with a question mark.

Root Words: Words before a suffix or prefix is added. Example: **write** is the root word of **rewritten**.

Sentences: A group of words that tell a complete idea or ask a question.

Short Vowels: The letters **a, e, i, o** and **u** which say the short sound. **Short a** is the sound you hear in **ant**. **Short e** is the sound you hear in **elephant**. **Short i** is the sound you hear in **igloo**. **Short o** is the sound you hear in **octopus**. **Short u** is the sound you hear in **umbrella**.

Singular: A noun that refers to only one thing.

Statements: Sentences that tell something. They begin with a capital letter and end with a period.

Suffixes: Word parts added to the ending of a word to change or add to its meaning. Example: state**ment**.

Verbs: Words that tell the action in a sentence. Example: The boy **ran** fast.

Vowels: The letters **a, e, i, o, u** and sometimes **y**.

Answer Keys

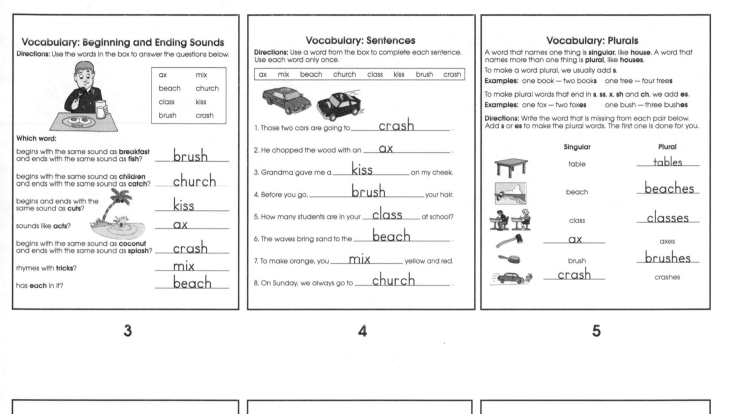

Vocabulary: Beginning and Ending Sounds

Directions: Use the words in the box to answer the questions below.

ax	mix
beach	church
class	kiss
brush	crash

Which word:

begins with the same sound as **breakfast** and ends with the same sound as **fish**? brush

begins with the same sound as **children** and ends with the same sound as **catch**? church

begins and ends with the same sound as **cuts**? kiss

sounds like **acts**? ax

begins with the same sound as **coconut** and ends with the same sound as **splash**? crash

rhymes with **tricks**? mix

has **each** in it? beach

3

Vocabulary: Sentences

Directions: Use a word from the box to complete each sentence. Use each word only once.

ax	mix	beach	church	class	kiss	brush	crash

1. Those two cars are going to crash .
2. He chopped the wood with an ax .
3. Grandma gave me a kiss on my cheek.
4. Before you go, brush your hair.
5. How many students are in your class at school?
6. The waves bring sand to the beach .
7. To make orange, you mix yellow and red.
8. On Sunday, we always go to church .

4

Vocabulary: Plurals

A word that names one thing is **singular**, like **house**. A word that names more than one thing is **plural**, like **houses**.
To make a word plural, we usually add **s**.
Examples: one book — two books   one tree — four trees
To make plural words that end in **s, ss, x, sh** and **ch**, we add **es**.
Examples: one fox — two fox**es**   one bush — three bush**es**
Directions: Write the word that is missing from each pair below. Add **s** or **es** to make the plural words. The first one is done for you.

	Singular	Plural
	table	tables
	beach	beaches
	class	classes
	ax	axes
	brush	brushes
	crash	crashes

5

Vocabulary: Spelling

Directions: Circle the word in each sentence which is not spelled correctly. Then write the word correctly.

1. How many (clases) are in your school? classes
2. Our town has six (chirches.) churches
3. Have you been to Maryland's (beechs?) beaches
4. Water (mixs) with dirt to make mud. mixes
5. We need two (axs) for this tree. axes
6. That car has been in three (crashs.) crashes
7. She gave the baby lots of (kises.) kisses
8. I lost both of my (brushs) at school. brushes

6

Vocabulary: Nouns and Verbs

A **noun** names a person, place or thing. A **verb** tells what something does or what something is. Some words can be a noun one time and a verb another time.

Directions: Complete each pair of sentences with a word from the box. The word will be a noun in the first sentence and a verb in the second sentence.

mix	kiss	brush	crash

1. Did your dog ever give you a kiss ?
   (noun)
   I have a cold, so I can't kiss you today.
   (verb)
2. I brought my comb and my brush .
   (noun)
   I will brush the leaves off your coat.
   (verb)
3. Was anyone hurt in the crash ?
   (noun)
   If you aren't careful, you will crash into me.
   (verb)
4. We bought a cake mix at the store.
   (noun)
   I will mix the eggs together.
   (verb)

7

Vocabulary: Nouns and Verbs

Directions: Write the correct word in each sentence. Use each word once. Write **N** above the words that are used as nouns (people, places and things). Write **V** above the words that are used as verbs (what something does or what something is).

Example:
I need a drink (N) . I will drink (V) milk.

mix	beach	church	class	kiss	brush	crash

1. It's hot today, so let's go to the beach (N) .
2. The church (N) was crowded.
3. I can't find my paint brush (N) .
4. Will you kiss (V) my finger and make it stop hurting?
5. I will mix (V) the red and yellow paint to get orange.
6. The teacher asked our class (N) to get in line.
7. If you move that bottom can, the rest will crash (V) to the floor.

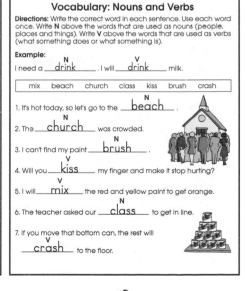

8

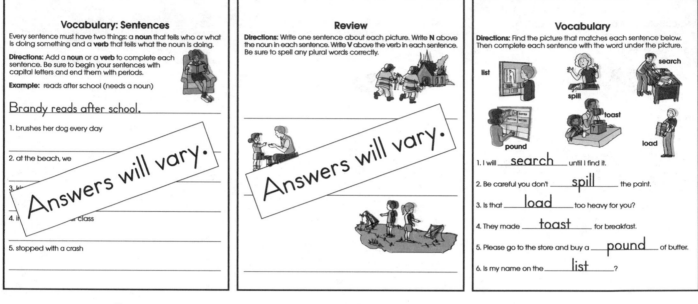

Vocabulary: Sentences

Every sentence must have two things: a **noun** that tells who or what is doing something and a **verb** that tells what the noun is doing.

Directions: Add a **noun** or a **verb** to complete each sentence. Be sure to begin your sentences with capital letters and end them with periods.

Example: reads after school (needs a noun)

Brandy reads after school.

1. brushes her dog every day

2. at the beach, we

3. k...

4. i... class

5. stopped with a crash

Answers will vary.

9

Review

Directions: Write one sentence about each picture. Write **N** above the noun in each sentence. Write **V** above the verb in each sentence. Be sure to spell any plural words correctly.

Answers will vary.

10

Vocabulary

Directions: Find the picture that matches each sentence below. Then complete each sentence with the word under the picture.

list   search   spill   toast   pound   load

1. I will __search__ until I find it.
2. Be careful you don't __spill__ the paint.
3. Is that __load__ too heavy for you?
4. They made __toast__ for breakfast.
5. Please go to the store and buy a __pound__ of butter.
6. Is my name on the __list__?

11

Vocabulary

Directions: Find the picture that matches each sentence below. Then complete the sentence with the word under the picture.

hug   plan   clap   stir   drag   grab

1. She will __plan__ where to go on her trip.
2. __Drag__ that big box over here, please.
3. My little brother always tries to __grab__ my toys.
4. May I help you __stir__ the soup?
5. I like to __hug__ my dog because he is so soft.
6. After she played, everyone started to __clap__.

12

Vocabulary: Word Puzzle

Directions: Look at the pictures below. Write the consonants they begin with on the lines. Then add vowels to spell words from the box.

c d h l n p r s t

pound   spill   toast   list   load   search

Example:

_c_ _p_ - _cup_

1. _l_ _s_ _t_ - _list_   4. _p_ _n_ _d_ - _pound_
2. _l_ _d_ - _load_   5. _t_ _s_ _t_ - _toast_
3. _s_ _r_ _c_ _h_ - _search_

13

Vocabulary: Adjectives

Adjectives are words that describe nouns. They often tell what kind, how many or what color.

Directions: Complete these sentences by writing nouns and adjectives. Then draw a picture to show what is happening in each sentence.

Example:

I caught __six__ __pink__ __pigs__.
       how many   what color   wh...

1. One day I hugged ___ ___ ___
   Answers will vary.   what

2. My brother dragged home ___ ___ ___
   how many   what color   what

14

© 1999 American Education Publishing Co.   **110**

Vocabulary: Beginning and Ending Sounds

Directions: Write the words from the box that begin or end with the same sound as the pictures.

| stir | clap | drag | hug | plan | grab |

1. Which word **begins** with the same sound as each picture?

2. Which word (or words) **ends** with the same sound as each picture.

clap   stir

hug   clap

grab   plan

drag   grab

stir   drag

plan   hug

15

Vocabulary: Explaining Sentences

Directions: Complete each sentence, explaining why each event might have happened.

She hugged me because _____

_____

He didn't want to play with us because _____

We planned to go to the ___

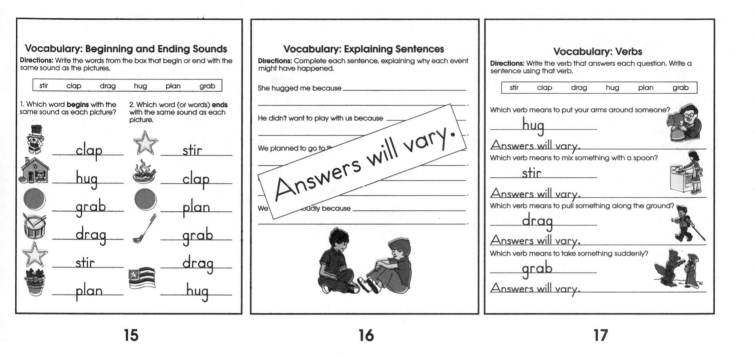

We ___ loudly because _____

Answers will vary.

16

Vocabulary: Verbs

Directions: Write the verb that answers each question. Write a sentence using that verb.

| stir | clap | drag | hug | plan | grab |

Which verb means to put your arms around someone?

hug

Answers will vary.

Which verb means to mix something with a spoon?

stir

Answers will vary.

Which verb means to pull something along the ground?

drag

Answers will vary.

Which verb means to take something suddenly?

grab

Answers will vary.

17

Vocabulary: Past-Tense Verbs

The past tense of a verb tells that something already happened. To tell about something that already happened, add **ed** to most verbs. If the verb already ends in **e**, just add **d**.

Examples:

We enter**ed** the contest last week.   We tast**ed** the cupcakes.
I fold**ed** the paper wrong.   They decid**ed** quickly.
He add**ed** two boxes to the pile.   She shar**ed** her cupcake.

Directions: Use the verb from the first sentence to complete the second sentence. Add **d** or **ed** to show that something already happened.

Example:

My mom looks fine today. Yesterday, she ___looked___ tired.

1. You enter through the middle door.
   We ___entered___ that way last week.

2. Please add this for me. I already ___added___ it twice.

3. Will you share your cookie with me?
   I ___shared___ my apple with you yesterday.

4. It's your turn to fold the clothes. I ___folded___ them yesterday.

5. May I taste another one? I already ___tasted___ one.

6. You need to decide. We ___decided___ this morning.

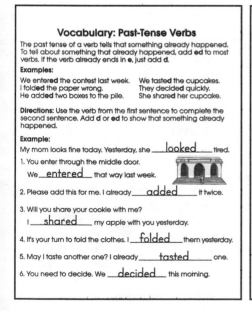

18

Vocabulary: Past-Tense Verbs

When you write about something that already happened, you add **ed** to most verbs. For some verbs that have a short vowel and end in one consonant, you double the consonant before adding **ed**.

Examples:

He hug**ged** his pillow.   The dog grab**bed** the stick.
She stir**red** the carrots.   We plan**ned** to go tomorrow.
They clap**ped** for me.   They drag**ged** their bags on the ground.

Directions: Use the verb from the first sentence to complete the second sentence. Change the verb in the second sentence to the past tense. Double the consonant and add **ed**.

Example:

We skip to school. Yesterday, we ___skipped___ the whole way.

1. It's not nice to grab things.
   When you ___grabbed___ my cookie, I felt angry.

2. Did anyone hug you today? Dad ___hugged___ me this morning.

3. We plan our vacations every year. Last year, we ___planned___ to go to the beach.

4. Is it my turn to stir the pot? You ___stirred___ it last time.

5. Let's clap for Andy, just like we ___clapped___ for Amy.

6. My sister used to drag her blanket everywhere.
   Once, she ___dragged___ it to the store.

19

Vocabulary: Past-Tense Verbs

When you write about something that already happened, you add **ed** to most verbs. Here is another way to write about something in the past tense.

Examples: The dog walked.   The dog was walking.
         The cats played.   The cats were playing.

Directions: Write each sentence again, writing the verb a different way.

Example: The baby pounded the pans.

The baby was pounding the pans.

1. Gary loaded the car by himself.

Gary was loading the car by himself.

2. They searched for a long time.

They were searching for a long time.

3. The water spilled over the edge.

The water was spilling over the edge.

4. Dad toasted the rolls.

Dad was toasting the rolls.

20

111

Vocabulary: Past-Tense Verbs

Directions: Write sentences that tell about each picture using the words **is**, **are**, **was** and **were**. Use words from the box as either nouns or verbs.

pound	spill	toast	list	load	search

Answers will vary.

21

Review

Directions: Read the questions below. Then write an answer to each question.

Pam's brother just won a singing contest. Pam and her family were watching. What do you think Pam and her parents did next?

Answers will vary.

...d wanted to give her dog a bath, but he wouldn't get into the water. He kept running away. What do you think Lisa finally did?

22

Review

Directions:

1. Read the sentence below. On another sheet of paper, write the rest of the story. Use **is**, **are**, **was** and **were** with some of your verbs.
2. Read your story out loud. Are your ideas clear? Did you ...ve anything out? Make any needed changes and ... story again.
3. Draw a picture to go with it.
4. Read your story to your f...

Sometime... ...ne day . . .

Answers will vary.

Dr...

Pictures will vary.

23

Vocabulary: Present-Tense Verbs

When something is happening right now, it is in the **present tense**. There are two ways to write verbs in the present tense:

Examples: The dog **walks**.   The cats **play**.
              The dog **is walking**.   The cats **are playing**.

Directions: Write each sentence again, writing the verb a different way.

Example:

He lists the numbers.
He is listing the numbers.

1. She is pounding the nail.
She pounds the nail.
2. My brother toasts the bread.
He is toasting the bread.
3. They search for the robber.
They are searching for the robber.
4. The teacher lists the pages.
The teacher is listing the pages.
5. They are spilling the water.
They spill the water.
6. Ken and Amy load the packages.
They are loading the packages.

24

Vocabulary: Sentences

Directions: Write a word from the box to complete each sentence. Use each word only once.

glue	enter	share	add	decide	fold

1. I know how to **add** 3 and 4.
2. Which book did you **decide** to read?
3. Go in the door that says " **Enter** ".
4. I will **glue** a yellow circle for the sun onto my picture.
5. I help **fold** the clothes after they are washed.
6. She will **share** her banana with me.

25

Vocabulary

Directions: Follow the directions below.

glue	enter	share	add	decide	fold

1. Add letters to these words to make words from the box.

old **fold**   are **share**

2. Write the two words from the box that begin with vowels.

enter   **add**

3. Change one letter of each word to make a word from the box.

food **fold**   clue **glue**

4. Change two letters of this word to make a word from the box.

beside **decide**

26

Vocabulary: Statements

A **statement** is a sentence that tells something.

Directions: Use the words in the box to complete the statements below. Write the words on the lines.

glue	decide	add
share	enter	fold

1. It took ten minutes for Kayla to ___add___ the numbers.

2. Ben wants to ___share___ his cookies with me.

3. "I can't ___decide___ which color to choose," said Rocky.

4. ___Glue___ can be used to make things stick together.

5. "This is how you ___fold___ your paper in half," said Mrs. Green.

6. The opposite of **leave** is ___enter___.

Write your own statement on the line.

Answers will vary.

27

Vocabulary: Questions

Questions are asking sentences. They begin with a capital letter and end with a question mark. Many questions begin with the words **who, what, why, when, where** and **how**. Write six questions using the question words below. Make sure to end each question with a question mark.

1. Who _____

2. What _____

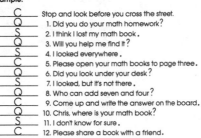

4. W

5. Where _____

6. How _____

28

Vocabulary: Commands

A **command** is a sentence that tells someone to do something.

Directions: Use the words in the box to complete the commands below. Write the words on the lines.

glue	decide	add	share	enter	fold

1. ___Add___ a cup of flour to the cake batter.

2. ___Decide___ how much paper you will need to write your story.

3. Please ___glue___ the picture of the apple onto the paper.

4. ___Enter___ through this door and leave through the other door.

5. Please ___fold___ the letter and put it into an envelope.

6. ___Share___ your toys with your sister.

Write your own command on the lines.

Answers will vary.

29

Vocabulary: Directions

A **direction** is a sentence written as a command.

Directions: Write the missing directions for these pictures. Begin each direction with one of the verbs below.

glue	enter	share	add	decide	fold

How To Make a Peanut Butter and Jelly Sandwich:

1. Spread peanut butter on bread.

2. _____

3. Cut th...

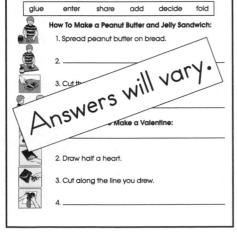

...o Make a Valentine:

2. Draw half a heart.

3. Cut along the line you drew.

4. _____

30

Kinds of Sentences

A **statement** is a sentence that tells something.
A **question** is a sentence that asks something.
A **command** is a sentence that tells someone to do something.

Commands begin with a verb or **please**. They usually end with a period. The noun is **you** but does not need to be part of the sentence.

Example: "Come here, please." means "You come here, please."

Examples of commands: Stand next to me.
Please give me some paper.

Directions: Write **S** in front of the statements, **Q** in front of the questions and **C** in front of the commands. End each sentence with a period or a question mark.

Example:

___C___ Stop and look before you cross the street.

___Q___ 1. Did you do your math homework?

___S___ 2. I think I lost my math book.

___Q___ 3. Will you help me find it?

___S___ 4. I looked everywhere.

___C___ 5. Please open your math books to page three.

___Q___ 6. Did you look under your desk?

___S___ 7. I looked, but it's not there.

___Q___ 8. Who can add seven and four?

___C___ 9. Come up and write the answer on the board.

___Q___ 10. Chris, where is your math book?

___S___ 11. I don't know for sure.

___C___ 12. Please share a book with a friend.

31

Kinds of Sentences

Remember: a **statement** tells something, a **question** asks something and a **command** tells someone to do something.

Directions: On each line, write a statement, question or command. Use a word from the box in each sentence.

glue	share	decide
enter	add	fold

Example:
Question:
Can he add anything else?

1. Statement:

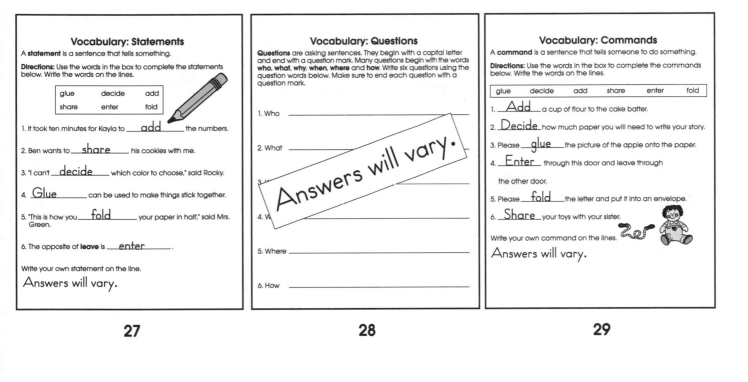

2. Quest...

3. ...

4. Statement:

5. Question:

32

113

Kinds of Sentences

Directions: Use the group of words below to write three sentences: a **statement**, a **question** and a **command**.

add	can	these	he	quickly	numbers

Example:

Statement:

He can add these numbers quickly.

Question:

Can he can add these numbers quickly?

Command:

Add these numbers quickly.

fold	here	should

1. Statement:

2. Question:

3. Command:

Answers will vary.

33

Vocabulary: Completing a Story

Directions: Use verbs to complete the story below. The verbs that tell about things that happened in the past will end in **ed**.

Answers may vary.

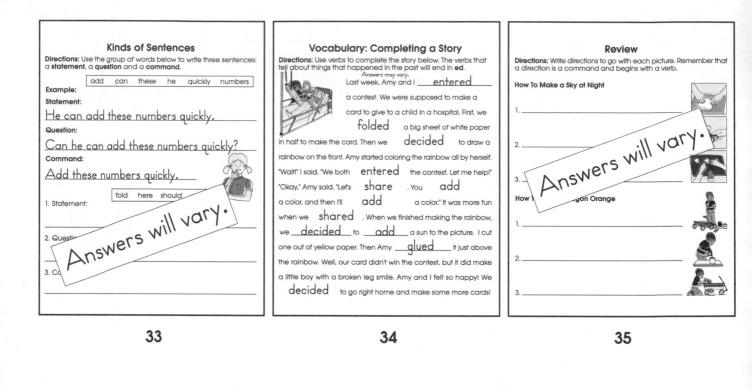

Last week, Amy and I ____entered____ a contest. We were supposed to make a card to give to a child in a hospital. First, we ____folded____ a big sheet of white paper in half to make the card. Then we ____decided____ to draw a rainbow on the front. Amy started coloring the rainbow all by herself. "Wait!" I said. "We both ____entered____ the contest. Let me help!" "Okay," Amy said. "Let's ____share____. You ____add____ a color, and then I'll ____add____ a color." It was more fun when we ____shared____. When we finished making the rainbow, we ____decided____ to ____add____ a sun to the picture. I cut one out of yellow paper. Then Amy ____glued____ it just above the rainbow. Well, our card didn't win the contest, but it did make a little boy with a broken leg smile. Amy and I felt so happy! We ____decided____ to go right home and make some more cards!

34

Review

Directions: Write directions to go with each picture. Remember that a direction is a command and begins with a verb.

How To Make a Sky at Night

1. _____

2. _____

3. _____

How T____ ____gon Orange

1. _____

2. _____

3. _____

Answers will vary.

35

Homophones

Homophones are words that sound the same but are spelled differently and have different meanings.

Directions: Use the homophones in the box to answer the riddles below.

main	meat	peace	dear	to
mane	meet	piece	deer	too

1. Which word has the word **pie** in it? ____piece____
2. Which word rhymes with **ear** and is an animal? ____deer____
3. Which word rhymes with **shoe** and means also? ____too____
4. Which word has the word **eat** in it and is something you might eat? ____meat____
5. Which word has the same letters as the word **read** but in a different order? ____dear____
6. Which word rhymes with **train** and is something on a pony? ____mane____
7. Which word, if it began with a capital letter, might be the name of an important street? ____main____
8. Which word sounds like a number but has only two letters? ____to____
9. Which word rhymes with and is a synonym for **greet**? ____meet____
10. Which word rhymes with the last syllable in **police** and can mean quiet? ____peace____

36

Homophones

Directions: Cut out each honeybee at the bottom of the page and glue it on the flower with its homophone.

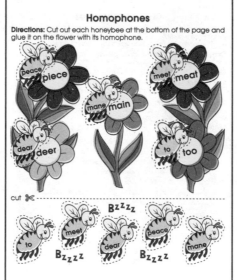

cut ✂ -

37

Homophones: Sentences

Directions: Write a word from the box to complete each sentence.

main	meat	peace	dear	two
mane	meet	piece	deer	too

1. The horse had a long, beautiful ____mane____.

   The ____main____ idea of the paragraph was boats.

2. Let's ____meet____ at my house to do our homework.

   The lion was fed ____meat____ at mealtime.

3. We had ____two____ kittens.

   Mike has a red bike. Tom does, ____too____.

4. The ____deer____ ran in front of the car.

   I begin my letters with "____Dear____ Mom."

39

Homophones: Spelling

Directions: Circle the word in each sentence which is not spelled correctly. Then write the word correctly.

1. Please (meat) me at the park. _____ meet _____

2. I would like a (peace) of pie. _____ piece _____

3. There were (too) cookies left. _____ two _____

4. The horse's (main) needed to be brushed. _____ mane _____

5. We saw a (dear) in the forest. _____ deer _____

40

Homophones: Rhymes

Directions: Use homophones to create two-lined rhymes.

Example: I found it a **pain**
To comb the horse's **mane**!

1. _____
_____

2. _____
_____ *Answers will vary.*

3. _____
_____

41

Review

Directions: Write two statements about the picture, one command and one question.

Statements:

1. _____

2. _____

Question: _____ *Answers will vary.*

Command: _____

42

Short Vowels

Short vowel patterns usually have a single vowel followed by a consonant sound.

Short a is the sound you hear in the word **can**.
Short e is the sound you hear in the word **men**.
Short i is the sound you hear in the word **pig**.
Short o is the sound you hear in the word **pot**.
Short u is the sound you hear in the word **truck**.

fast	stop
spin	track
wish	lunch
bread	block

Directions: Use the words in the box to answer the questions below.

Which word:

begins with the same sound as **blast** and ends with the same sound as **look**? _____ block _____

rhymes with **stack**? _____ track _____

begins with the same sound as **phone** and ends with the same sound as **lost**? _____ fast _____

has the same vowel sound as **hen**? _____ bread _____

rhymes with **crunch**? _____ lunch _____

begins with the same sound as **spot** and ends with the same sound as **can**? _____ spin _____

begins with the same sound as **win** and ends with the same sound as **crush**? _____ wish _____

has the word **top** in it? _____ stop _____

43

Short Vowels: Sentences

Directions: Use the words in the box to complete each sentence.

fast	wish	truck	bread	sun
best	stop	track	lunch	block

Race cars can go very _____ fast

Carol packs a _____ lunch _____ for Ted before school.

Throw a penny in the well and make a _____ wish

The _____ truck _____ had a flat tire.

My favorite kind of _____ bread _____ is whole wheat.

44

Short Vowels: Spelling

Directions: Circle the word in each sentence which is not spelled correctly. Then write the word correctly.

1. Be sure to (stopp) at the red light. _____ stop _____

2. The train goes down the (trak). _____ track _____

3. Please put the (bred) in the toaster. _____ bread _____

4. I need another (blok) to finish. _____ block _____

5. The (beasst) player won a trophy. _____ best _____

6. Blow out the candles and make a (wish). _____ wish _____

7. The (truk) blew its horn. _____ truck _____

45

Review

Directions: Write one sentence about each picture. Be sure to begin each sentence with a capital letter and end it with a period.

Answers will vary.

46

Long Vowels

Long vowels are the letters **a, e, i, o** and **u** which say the letter name sound.

Long a is the sound you hear in **cane**.
Long e is the sound you hear in **green**.
Long i is the sound you hear in **pie**.
Long o is the sound you hear in **bowl**.
Long u is the sound you hear in **cube**.

lame	goal
pain	few
street	fright
nose	gray
bike	fuse

Directions: Use the words in the box to answer the questions below.

1. Add one letter to each of these words to make words from the box.

ray __gray__   use __fuse__   right __fright__

2. Change one letter from each word to make a word from the box.

pall __pain__   goat __goal__
late __lame__   bite __bike__

3. Write the word from the box that . . .

has the long **e** sound. __street__
rhymes with **you**. __few__
is a homophone for **knows**. __nose__

47

Long Vowels: Sentences

Directions: Use the words in the box to complete each sentence.

lame	goal	pain	few	bike
street	fright	nose	gray	fuse

1. Look both ways before crossing the __street__ .

2. My __bike__ had a flat tire.

3. Our walk through the haunted house gave us such a __fright__ .

4. I kicked the soccer ball and scored a __goal__ .

5. The __gray__ clouds mean rain is coming.

6. Cover your __nose__ when you sneeze.

7. We blew a __fuse__ at my house last night.

48

Long Vowels

Directions: Use long vowel words from the box to answer the clues below. Write the letters of the words on the lines.

few	bike	dime	goal	fuse	lame	street	nose	fright	pain

1. f r i g h t (rhymes with **night**)
2. s t r e e t (could be Main or Maple)
3. f e w (synonym for **a couple**)
4. l a m e (rhymes with **tame**)
5. b i k e (can be ridden on a trail)
6. p a i n (homophone for **pane**)
7. d i m e (ten of these make a dollar)
8. g o a l (changing one letter of this word makes **goat**)
9. f u s e (has the word **use** in it)
10. n o s e (homophone for **knows**)

Now, read the letters in the boxes from top to bottom to find out what kind of a job you did! __tremendous__

49

Review

Directions: Imagine that you are a puppy outside. What would you do and see? Write sentences below to tell what you would do and see.

Answers will vary.

50

Adjectives

Directions: Use the words in the box to answer the questions below. Use each word only once.

polite	careless	neat	shy	selfish	thoughtful

1. Someone who is quiet and needs some time to make new friends is __shy__ .

2. A person who says "please" and "thank you" is __polite__ .

3. Someone who always puts all the toys away is __neat__ .

4. A person who won't share with others is being __selfish__ .

5. A person who leaves a bike out all night is being __careless__ .

6. Someone who thinks of others is __thoughtful__ .

51

Adjectives

Directions: Use the adjectives in the box to answer the questions below.

| polite | careless | neat | shy | selfish | thoughtful |

1. Change a letter in each word to make an adjective.

near   neat

why   shy

2. Write the word that rhymes with each of these.

fell dish   selfish

not full   thoughtful

hair mess   careless

3. Find these words in the adjectives. Write the adjective.

at   neat

are   careless

it   polite

52

Adjectives: Spelling

Directions: Circle the word in each sentence which is not spelled correctly. Then write the word correctly.

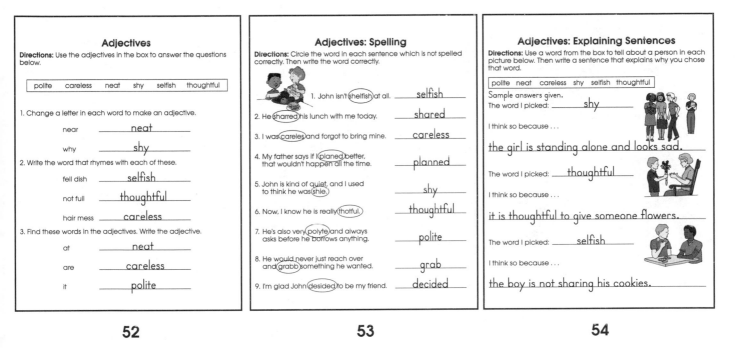

1. John isn't (shelfish) at all.   selfish

2. He (sharred) his lunch with me today.   shared

3. I was (careles) and forgot to bring mine.   careless

4. My father says if I (planed) better, that wouldn't happen all the time.   planned

5. John is kind of quiet, and I used to think he was (shie.)   shy

6. Now, I know he is really (thotful.)   thoughtful

7. He's also very (polyte) and always asks before he borrows anything.   polite

8. He would never just reach over and (grabb) something he wanted.   grab

9. I'm glad John (desided) to be my friend.   decided

53

Adjectives: Explaining Sentences

Directions: Use a word from the box to tell about a person in each picture below. Then write a sentence that explains why you chose that word.

| polite | neat | careless | shy | selfish | thoughtful |

Sample answers given.

The word I picked: _____ shy

I think so because . . .

the girl is standing alone and looks sad.

The word I picked: _____ thoughtful

I think so because . . .

it is thoughtful to give someone flowers.

The word I picked: _____ selfish

I think so because . . .

the boy is not sharing his cookies.

54

Adjectives

Directions: Look at each picture. Then add adjectives to the sentences. Use colors, numbers, words from the box and any other words you need to describe each picture.

Example:

The boy shared his pencil.

| polite | neat | careless |
| shy | selfish | thoughtful |

The polite boy shared his red pencil.

The girl dropped her coat.

The boy pl_____

The boy put books away.

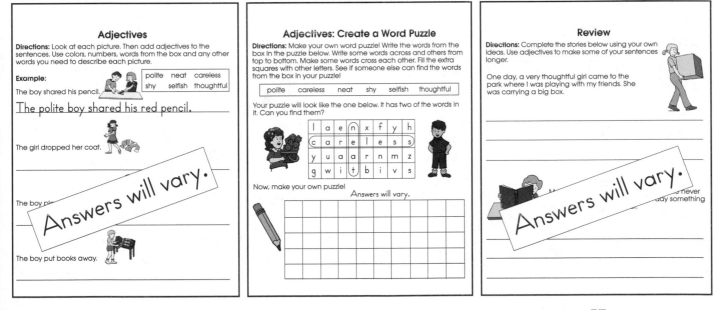

Answers will vary.

55

Adjectives: Create a Word Puzzle

Directions: Make your own word puzzle! Write the words from the box in the puzzle below. Write some words across and others from top to bottom. Make some words cross each other. Fill the extra squares with other letters. See if someone else can find the words from the box in your puzzle!

| polite | careless | neat | shy | selfish | thoughtful |

Your puzzle will look like the one below. It has two of the words in it. Can you find them?

l	a	e	n	x	f	y	h
c	a	r	e	l	e	s	s
y	u	a	a	r	n	m	z
g	w	i	t	b	i	v	s

Now, make your own puzzle!

Answers will vary.

56

Review

Directions: Complete the stories below using your own ideas. Use adjectives to make some of your sentences longer.

One day, a very thoughtful girl came to the park where I was playing with my friends. She was carrying a big box.

Answers will vary.

57

117

C, K, CK Words: Spelling

Directions: Write the words from the box that answer the questions.

crowd	keeper	cost	pack	kangaroo	thick

1. Which words spell the **k** sound with a **k**?

keeper   kangaroo

2. Which words spell the **k** sound with a **c**?

crowd   cost

3. Which words spell the **k** sound with **ck**?

pack   thick

4. Circle the letters that spell **k** in these words:

(co)o(k)   bla(ck)   (c)ool   (k)ite
(c)ake   po(ck)et   po(k)e

5. Which words from the box rhyme with each of these?

tossed   cost   deeper   keeper

proud   crowd   all in blue   kangaroo

58

C, K, CK Words: Sentences

The **k** sound can be spelled with a **c**, **k** or **ck** after a short vowel sound.

Directions: Use the words from the box to complete the sentences. Use each word only once.

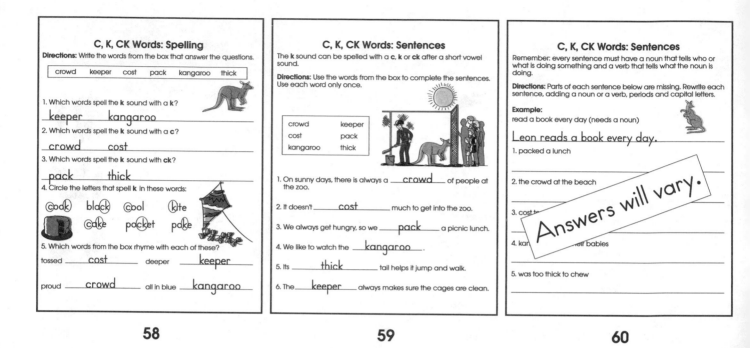

crowd	keeper
cost	pack
kangaroo	thick

1. On sunny days, there is always a ___crowd___ of people at the zoo.

2. It doesn't ___cost___ much to get into the zoo.

3. We always get hungry, so we ___pack___ a picnic lunch.

4. We like to watch the ___kangaroo___ .

5. Its ___thick___ tail helps it jump and walk.

6. The ___keeper___ always makes sure the cages are clean.

59

C, K, CK Words: Sentences

Remember: every sentence must have a noun that tells who or what is doing something and a verb that tells what the noun is doing.

Directions: Parts of each sentence below are missing. Rewrite each sentence, adding a noun or a verb, periods and capital letters.

Example:
read a book every day (needs a noun)

Leon reads a book every day.

1. packed a lunch

2. the crowd at the beach

3. cost t~~

Answers will vary.

4. kar~~ ~~eir babies

5. was too thick to chew

60

C, K, CK Words: Joining Sentences

Joining words are words that make two sentences into one longer sentence. Here are some words that join sentences:

and — if both sentences are about the same noun or verb.
   Example: Tom is in my class at school, **and** he lives near me.
but — if the second sentence says something different from the first sentence.
   Example: Julie walks to school with me, **but** today she is sick.
or — if each sentence names a different thing you could do.
   Example: We could go to my house, **or** we could go to yours.

Directions: Join each set of sentences below using the words **and**, **but** or **or**.

1. Those socks usually cost a lot. This pack of ten socks is cheaper.

Those socks usually cost a lot, but this pack of ten socks is cheaper.

2. The kangaroo has a pouch. It lives in Australia.

The kangaroo has a pouch, and it lives in Australia.

3. The zoo keeper can start to work early. She can stay late.

The zoo keeper can start to work early, or she can stay late.

61

C, K, CK Words: Joining Sentences

If and **when** can be joining words, too.

Directions: Read each set of sentences. Then join the two sentences to make one longer sentence.

Example: The apples will need to be washed. The apples are dirty.

The apples will need to be washed if they are dirty.

1. The size of the crowd grew. It grew when the game began.

The size of the crowd grew when the game began.

2. Be careful driving in the fog. The fog is thick.

Be careful driving in the fog if the fog is thick.

3. Pack your suitcases. Do it when you wake up in the morning.

Pack your suitcases when you wake up in the morning.

62

C, K, CK Words: Joining Sentences

Other words that can join sentences are:

when — **When** we got there, the show had already started.
after — **After** I finished my homework, I watched TV.
because — You can't go by yourself, **because** you are too young.

Directions: Use the joining words to make the two short sentences into one longer one.

1. *when* The keeper opened the door. The bear got out.

When the keeper opened the door, the bear got out.

2. *because* I didn't buy the tickets. They cost too much.

I didn't buy the tickets because they cost too much.

3. *after* The kangaroo ate lunch. He took a nap.

After the kangaroo ate lunch, he took a nap.

4. *when* The door opened. The crowd rushed in.

When the door opened, the crowd rushed in.

5. *after* I cut the bread. Everyone had a slice.

After I cut the bread, everyone had a slice.

63

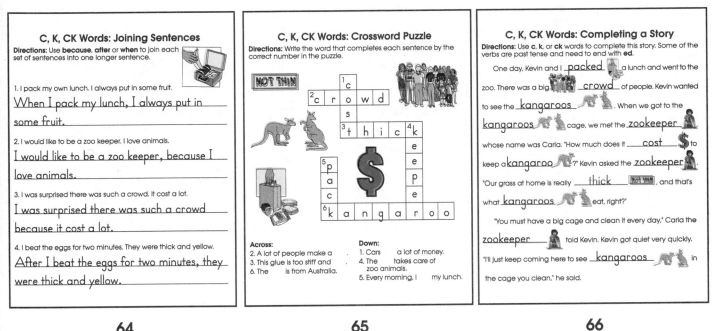

C, K, CK Words: Joining Sentences

Directions: Use **because**, **after** or **when** to join each set of sentences into one longer sentence.

1. I pack my own lunch. I always put in some fruit.

When I pack my lunch, I always put in some fruit.

2. I would like to be a zoo keeper. I love animals.

I would like to be a zoo keeper, because I love animals.

3. I was surprised there was such a crowd. It cost a lot.

I was surprised there was such a crowd because it cost a lot.

4. I beat the eggs for two minutes. They were thick and yellow.

After I beat the eggs for two minutes, they were thick and yellow.

64

C, K, CK Words: Crossword Puzzle

Directions: Write the word that completes each sentence by the correct number in the puzzle.

NOT THIN

2. c r o w d
   1. c
      s
   3. t h i c 4. k
                  e
                  e
   5. p   p
      a   e
      c
   6. k a n g a r o o

Across:
2. A lot of people make a
3. This glue is too stiff and
6. The ___ is from Australia.

Down:
1. Cars ___ a lot of money.
4. The ___ takes care of zoo animals.
5. Every morning, I ___ my lunch.

65

C, K, CK Words: Completing a Story

Directions: Use **c**, **k**, or **ck** words to complete this story. Some of the verbs are past tense and need to end with **ed**.

One day, Kevin and I packed a lunch and went to the zoo. There was a big crowd of people. Kevin wanted to see the kangaroos. When we got to the kangaroos cage, we met the zookeeper whose name was Carla. "How much does it cost $ to keep a kangaroo?" Kevin asked the zookeeper.

"Our grass at home is really thick, and that's what kangaroos eat, right?"

"You must have a big cage and clean it every day," Carla the zookeeper told Kevin. Kevin got quiet very quickly.

"I'll just keep coming here to see kangaroos in the cage you clean," he said.

66

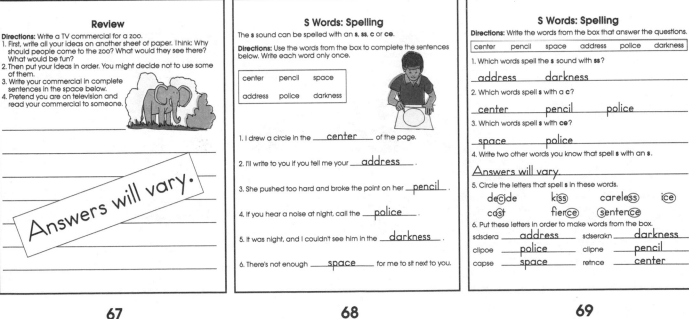

Review

Directions: Write a TV commercial for a zoo.
1. First, write all your ideas on another sheet of paper. Think: Why should people come to the zoo? What would they see there? What would be fun?
2. Then put your ideas in order. You might decide not to use some of them.
3. Write your commercial in complete sentences in the space below.
4. Pretend you are on television and read your commercial to someone.

Answers will vary.

67

S Words: Spelling

The **s** sound can be spelled with an **s**, **ss**, **c** or **ce**.

Directions: Use the words from the box to complete the sentences below. Write each word only once.

| center | pencil | space |
| address | police | darkness |

1. I drew a circle in the center of the page.

2. I'll write to you if you tell me your address.

3. She pushed too hard and broke the point on her pencil.

4. If you hear a noise at night, call the police.

5. It was night, and I couldn't see him in the darkness.

6. There's not enough space for me to sit next to you.

68

S Words: Spelling

Directions: Write the words from the box that answer the questions.

| center | pencil | space | address | police | darkness |

1. Which words spell the **s** sound with **ss**?

address   darkness

2. Which words spell **s** with a **c**?

center   pencil   police

3. Which words spell **s** with **ce**?

space   police

4. Write two other words you know that spell **s** with an **s**.

Answers will vary.

5. Circle the letters that spell **s** in these words.

de(c)ide   ki(ss)   carele(ss)   i(ce)
co(s)t   fier(ce)   (s)enten(ce)

6. Put these letters in order to make words from the box.

sdsdera address   sdserakn darkness
clipoe   police   clipne   pencil
capse   space   retnce   center

69

S Words: Sentences

Directions: Write your own sentences using the word pairs below.

Example: class   share

In my class at school, we all

share the work.

1. decide   center

_____

_____

2. space   address

_____

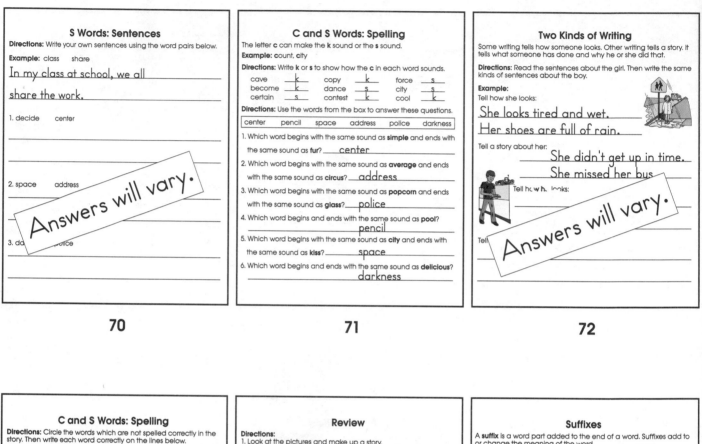

3. d_____ police

_____

_____

70

C and S Words: Spelling

The letter **c** can make the **k** sound or the **s** sound.

Example: count, city

Directions: Write **k** or **s** to show how the **c** in each word sounds.

cave	k	copy	k	force	s
become	k	dance	s	city	s
certain	s	contest	k	cool	k

Directions: Use the words from the box to answer these questions.

center	pencil	space	address	police	darkness

1. Which word begins with the same sound as **simple** and ends with the same sound as **fur**? _____ center

2. Which word begins with the same sound as **average** and ends with the same sound as **circus**? address

3. Which word begins with the same sound as **popcorn** and ends with the same sound as **glass**? _____ police

4. Which word begins and ends with the same sound as **pool**? _____ pencil

5. Which word begins with the same sound as **city** and ends with the same sound as **kiss**? _____ space

6. Which word begins and ends with the same sound as **delicious**? _____ darkness

71

Two Kinds of Writing

Some writing tells how someone looks. Other writing tells a story. It tells what someone has done and why he or she did that.

Directions: Read the sentences about the girl. Then write the same kinds of sentences about the boy.

Example:

Tell how she looks:

She looks tired and wet.
Her shoes are full of rain.

Tell a story about her:

She didn't get up in time.
She missed her bus

Tell how he looks:

Tell

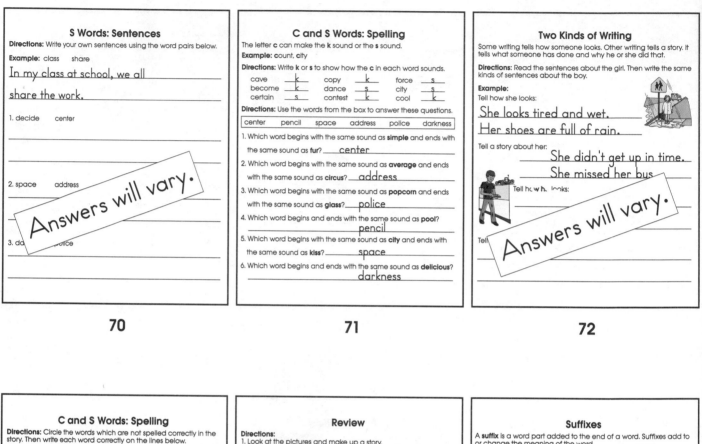

72

C and S Words: Spelling

Directions: Circle the words which are not spelled correctly in the story. Then write each word correctly on the lines below.

One day, Peter and I were sitting on a bench at the park. A polise woman came and sat in the empty spase beside us. "Have you seen a little dog with thik black fur?" she asked. She was very poolite. "Remember that dog?" I asked Peter. "He was just here!" Peter nodded. He was too shie to say anything.

"Give us his adress," I said. "We'll find him and take him home." She got out a pensil and wrote the address in the senter of a piece of paper. Peter and I desided to walk down the street the way the dog had gone. There was a krowd of people at a cherch we passed, but no dog.

Then it started getting late. "We better go home," Peter said. "I can't see in this drakness anyway."

As we turned around to go back, there was the little dog! He had been following us! We took him to the adress. The girl who came to the door grabed him and hugged him tight. "I'm sorry I let you wander away," she told the dog. "I'll never be so carless again." I thought she was going to kis us, too. We left just in time!

police	space	thick
polite	shy	address
pencil	address	center
decided	crowd	church
darkness	address	grabbed
hugged	careless	kiss

73

Review

Directions:
1. Look at the pictures and make up a story.
2. Write the story in sentences on another sheet of paper. Do your sentences tell what happened in the order it happened? Does each sentence have a noun and a verb? Did you combine some short sentences with **or, and, but, because, when** or **after**?
3. Read your story to someone. Are there any changes that would make your story clearer?
4. Copy your story in the space under the pictures.
5. Then read your story to someone else.

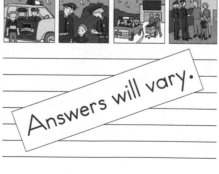

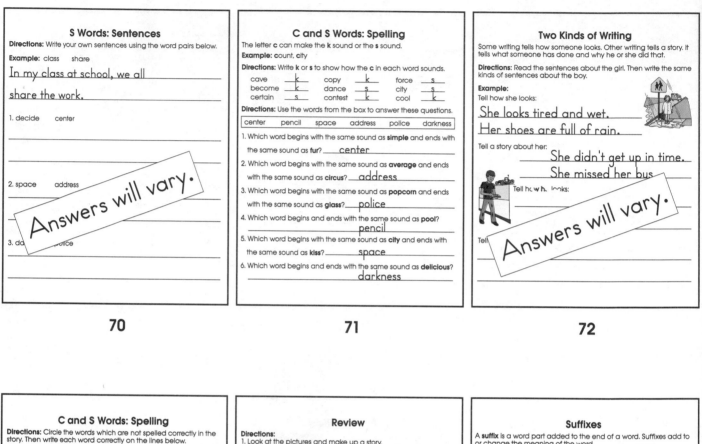

74

Suffixes

A **suffix** is a word part added to the end of a word. Suffixes add to or change the meaning of the word.

Example: sad + ly = sadly

Below are some suffixes and their meanings.

ment	state of being, quality of, act of
ly	like or in a certain way
ness	state of being
ful	full of
less	without

Directions: The words in the box have suffixes. Use the suffix meanings above to match each word with its meaning below. Write the words on the lines.

friendly	cheerful	safely	sleeveless	speechless
kindness	amazement	sickness	peaceful	excitement

1. in a safe way   s a f e l y
2. full of cheer   c h e e r f u l
3. full of peace   p e a c e f u l
4. state of being amazed a m a z e m e n t
5. state of being excited e x c i t e m e n t
6. without speech   s p e e c h l e s s

Use the numbered letters to find the missing word below.

You are now on your way to becoming a

m a s t e r of suffixes!

75

Suffixes: Adverbs

Answers will vary.

Adverbs are words that describ_____ ___ell where, when or how. Most adverbs e_____

Directions: Com_____ _____e with the correct part of speech.

Example:

Hank	wrote	here.
who? (noun)	what? (verb)	where? (adverb)

1.
	was lost	
who? (noun)	what? (verb)	where? (adverb)

2.
		quickly.
who? (noun)	what? (verb)	how? (adverb)

3.
	felt	
who? (noun)	what? (verb)	how? (adverb)

4.
My brother		
who? (noun)	what? (verb)	when? (adverb)

5.
	woke up	
who? (noun)	what? (verb)	when? (adverb)

6.
		gladly.
who? (noun)	what? (verb)	how? (adverb)

76

Suffixes: Root Words

A **root word** is a word before a suffix is added.

Example: In the word **hope**ful, the root word is **hope**.

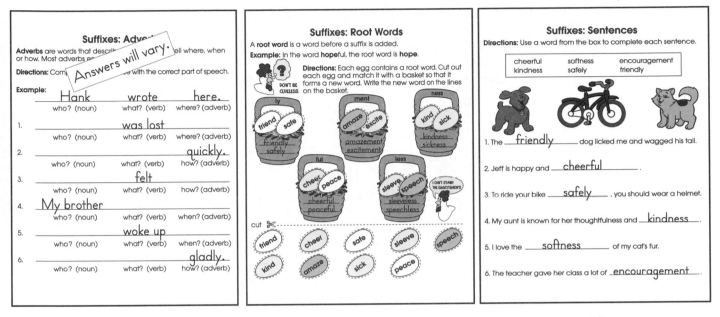

Directions: Each egg contains a root word. Cut out each egg and match it with a basket so that it forms a new word. Write the new word on the lines on the basket.

DON'T BE CLUELESS!

ly — friend, safe — friendly, safely

ment — amaze, excite — amazement, excitement

ness — kind, sick — kindness, sickness

ful — cheer, peace — cheerful, peaceful

less — sleeve, speech — sleeveless, speechless

I CAN'T STAND THE EGGCITEMENT!

cut ✂ - - - - - -

friend · cheer · safe · sleeve · speech

kind · amaze · sick · peace

77

Suffixes: Sentences

Directions: Use a word from the box to complete each sentence.

cheerful	softness	encouragement
kindness	safely	friendly

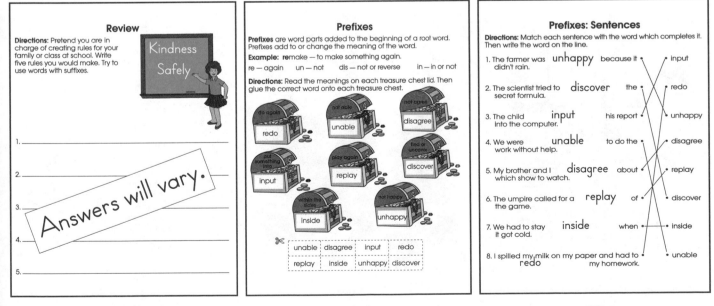

1. The ___friendly___ dog licked me and wagged his tail.

2. Jeff is happy and ___cheerful___ .

3. To ride your bike ___safely___ , you should wear a helmet.

4. My aunt is known for her thoughtfulness and ___kindness___ .

5. I love the ___softness___ of my cat's fur.

6. The teacher gave her class a lot of ___encouragement___

79

Review

Directions: Pretend you are in charge of creating rules for your family or class at school. Write five rules you would make. Try to use words with suffixes.

Kindness
Safely

1. _____

2. _____

Answers will vary.

3. _____

4. _____

5. _____

80

Prefixes

Prefixes are word parts added to the beginning of a root word. Prefixes add to or change the meaning of the word.

Example: **re**make — to make something again.

re — again   un — not   dis — not or reverse   in — in or not

Directions: Read the meanings on each treasure chest lid. Then glue the correct word onto each treasure chest.

do again — redo

not able — unable

not agree — disagree

put something into — input

play again — replay

find or uncover — discover

within the sides — inside

not happy — unhappy

✂

unable	disagree	input	redo
replay	inside	unhappy	discover

81

Prefixes: Sentences

Directions: Match each sentence with the word which completes it. Then write the word on the line.

1. The farmer was ___unhappy___ because it didn't rain.   • input

2. The scientist tried to ___discover___ the secret formula.   • redo

3. The child ___input___ his report into the computer.   • unhappy

4. We were ___unable___ to do the work without help.   • disagree

5. My brother and I ___disagree___ about which show to watch.   • replay

6. The umpire called for a ___replay___ of the game.   • discover

7. We had to stay ___inside___ when it got cold.   • inside

8. I spilled my milk on my paper and had to ___redo___ my homework.   • unable

83

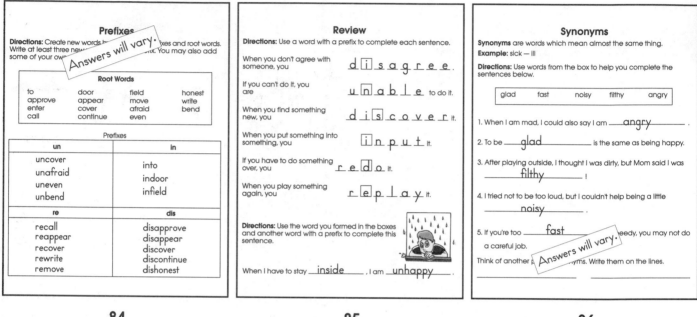

84

85

86

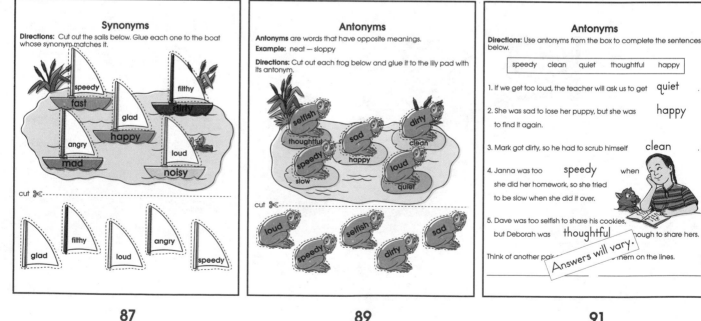

87

89

91

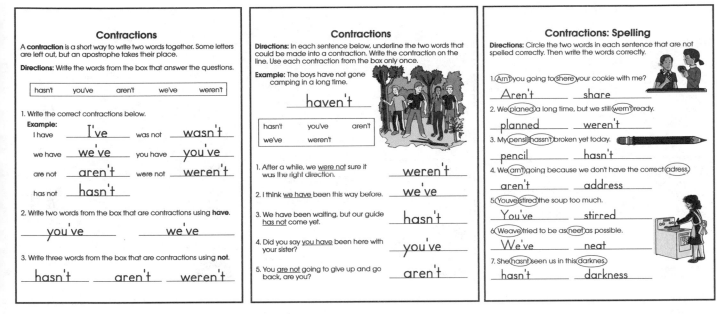

Contractions

A **contraction** is a short way to write two words together. Some letters are left out, but an apostrophe takes their place.

Directions: Write the words from the box that answer the questions.

| hasn't | you've | aren't | we've | weren't |

1. Write the correct contractions below.

Example:

I have   I've   was not   wasn't

we have   we've   you have   you've

are not   aren't   were not   weren't

has not   hasn't

2. Write two words from the box that are contractions using **have**.

you've   we've

3. Write three words from the box that are contractions using **not**.

hasn't   aren't   weren't

92

Contractions

Directions: In each sentence below, underline the two words that could be made into a contraction. Write the contraction on the line. Use each contraction from the box only once.

Example: The boys have not gone camping in a long time.

haven't

| hasn't | you've | aren't |
| we've | weren't | |

1. After a while, we were not sure it was the right direction.   weren't

2. I think we have been this way before.   we've

3. We have been waiting, but our guide has not come yet.   hasn't

4. Did you say you have been here with your sister?   you've

5. You are not going to give up and go back, are you?   aren't

93

Contractions: Spelling

Directions: Circle the two words in each sentence that are not spelled correctly. Then write the words correctly.

1. Arn't you going to shere your cookie with me?

Aren't   share

2. We planed a long time, but we still wern't ready.

planned   weren't

3. My pensil hasn't broken yet today.

pencil   hasn't

4. We arn't going because we don't have the correct adress.

aren't   address

5. Youve stired the soup too much.

You've   stirred

6. Weave tried to be as neet as possible.

We've   neat

7. She hasnt seen us in this darkness.

hasn't   darkness

94

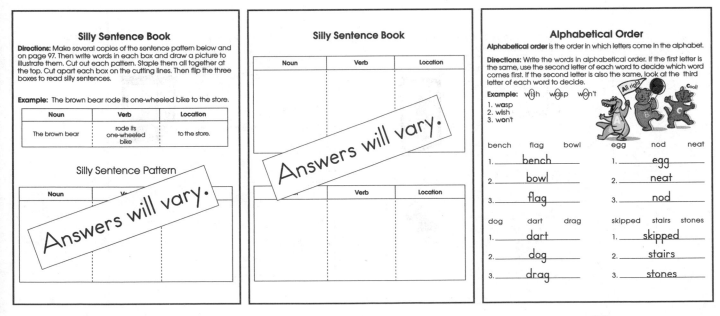

Silly Sentence Book

Directions: Make several copies of the sentence pattern below and on page 97. Then write words in each box and draw a picture to illustrate them. Cut out each pattern. Staple them all together at the top. Cut apart each box on the cutting lines. Then flip the three boxes to read silly sentences.

Example: The brown bear rode its one-wheeled bike to the store.

Noun	Verb	Location
The brown bear	rode its one-wheeled bike	to the store.

Silly Sentence Pattern

Noun	Verb	Location

Answers will vary.

95

Silly Sentence Book

Noun	Verb	Location

Answers will vary.

	Verb	Location

97

Alphabetical Order

Alphabetical order is the order in which letters come in the alphabet.

Directions: Write the words in alphabetical order. If the first letter is the same, use the second letter of each word to decide which word comes first. If the second letter is also the same, look at the third letter of each word to decide.

Example: wish   wasp   won't

1. wasp
2. wish
3. won't

bench   flag   bowl   egg   nod   neat

1. bench   1. egg

2. bowl   2. neat

3. flag   3. nod

dog   dart   drag   skipped   stairs   stones

1. dart   1. skipped

2. dog   2. stairs

3. drag   3. stones

99

Dictionary Skills

A **dictionary** is a book that tells how to pronounce and spell words and what words mean.

The words in a dictionary are in alphabetical order. That makes them easy to find. To look up a word, use the guide words. **Guide words** are at the top of each page. The word on the left is the first word listed on the page. The word on the right is the last word listed on the page.

Directions: Answer the questions about this dictionary page.

aardvark	atlas
aardvark — an animal that is much like an anteater	**apple** — a fruit
all — every one of something	**ark** — a large boat
ant — a small insect	**atlas** — a book of maps

1. What are the guide words on this page?   aardvark, atlas

2. What is an animal that is like an anteater?   aardvark

3. What is a type of boat?   ark

4. What is an atlas?   a book of maps

5. Which word is a kind of fruit?   apple

6. What is the last word on this dictionary page?   atlas

100

Dictionary Skills

Directions: Cross out the words in the box that would not belong on this page. Then write the rest of the words in alphabetical order on the blanks below.

octopus   quilt

octopus   part
old   pink
open   poor
orange   porch
order   quarrel
paint   quilt

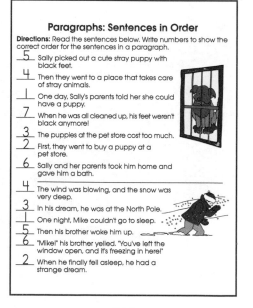

octopus	~~water~~	old	part
~~stairs~~	order	~~frog~~	quarrel
pink	paint	orange	poor
porch	~~oats~~	quilt	open

101

Paragraphs

A **paragraph** is a group of sentences that all tell about the same thing.

Directions: In each paragraph below, draw a line through the sentence that doesn't belong. Circle all the contractions.

We have a rule at our house. After you've done your homework, you can watch one TV show. ~~I walk home from school.~~ Tonight I don't have any homework, so I guess I can't watch TV.

In our class, we aren't allowed to chew gum. The teacher says he can tell when we've got gum in our mouths. He says it makes us look like cows. That hasn't stopped Jimmy, though. ~~He likes ice cream better.~~ He chews gum when the teacher isn't looking.

My sister and I weren't supposed to cut through the field on the way home from school today. ~~My friend Carla rides the bus home.~~ Now, I know why Mom told us not to do that. The field is full of mud—and so are our shoes!

We've got a dog named Pepper at our house. I feed Pepper every day, but my brother hasn't helped in a long time. ~~He's taller than I am.~~ I think Pepper likes me better than he likes my brother!

102

Paragraphs: Sentences in Order

Directions: Read the sentences below. Write numbers to show the correct order for the sentences in a paragraph.

5 Sally picked out a cute stray puppy with black feet.

4 Then they went to a place that takes care of stray animals.

1 One day, Sally's parents told her she could have a puppy.

7 When he was all cleaned up, his feet weren't black anymore!

3 The puppies at the pet store cost too much.

2 First, they went to buy a puppy at a pet store.

6 Sally and her parents took him home and gave him a bath.

4 The wind was blowing, and the snow was very deep.

3 In his dream, he was at the North Pole.

1 One night, Mike couldn't go to sleep.

5 Then his brother woke him up.

6 "Mike!" his brother yelled. "You've left the window open, and it's freezing in here!"

2 When he finally fell asleep, he had a strange dream.

103

Review

Directions: Follow the steps below to write a paragraph about this picture. Your paragraph could tell what you see in the picture or you could make up a story about what is happening here.

1. First, write all your ideas on another sheet of paper.
2. Choose the ideas you want to use in your paragraph. Leave out the ones that don't belong.
3. Put your ideas in order so they make sense.
4. Write them in sentences on another sheet of paper.
5. Read your sentences to someone and ask if you need to make any changes.
6. After you make the changes, write your paragraph below.

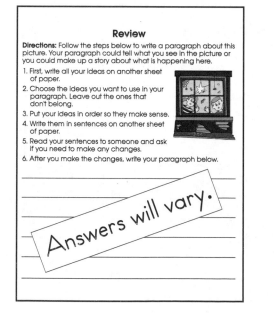

Answers will vary.

104

Research Project

Directions: Choose any animal that interests you. What kinds of things do you already know about this animal? What do you want to find out about it?

This research project will help you organize the facts you find and use them to write a paragraph.

First, find information about your animal. Use an encyclopedia, a special book about the animal or the Internet. Write your facts here.

Example:

Animal: the tuatara, a lizard-like creature

Where does it live? lives only on small, chilly islands off New Zealand

Animal:

Where does it live?

What does it eat and how does it catch or eat its food?

Describe in detail what it looks like.

Other interesting facts:

105

Research Project

Use the facts you researched to write sentences for a paragraph. Indent the first word.

Sample first sentence:

The tuatara is an interesting lizard-like creature.

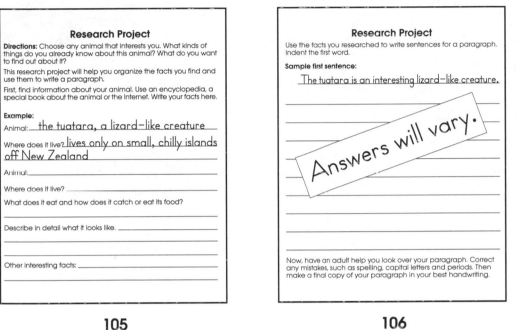

Answers will vary.

Now, have an adult help you look over your paragraph. Correct any mistakes, such as spelling, capital letters and periods. Then make a final copy of your paragraph in your best handwriting.

106

Teaching Suggestions

Review with your child how to study a word:
1) Look at the word.
2) Say the word.
3) Write the word.
4) Check yourself.

Repeat the steps if the word is incorrect.

Other things to do besides write a word for practice:
- Chant the spelling.
- Write the word in the air.
- Use frosting or a condiment to write the word on food.
- Fill an empty mustard container with water and write the words on your sidewalk or driveway.
- Write the word in the snow with a stick or umbrella.
- Put the word to a song (i.e., sing the tune of **Bingo** for a 5-letter word).
- Spell the word aloud, tapping on consonants, clapping on vowels.

Every day, write one sentence with errors in it. Have your child correct it. Focus on spelling, punctuation, capitalization and word order. **Example:** the dag and cat fite.

Help your child create his/her own spelling dictionary.

Have a word poster or folder for your child to keep a list of new words.

Then he/she can study and review the words independently.

Teach your child more words with multiple meanings using a dictionary. For example, you could look up the word **bat** and discuss the different meanings of the word.

Have your child keep a daily writing journal.

Write cartoons together. Cartoons provide writing practice using frames, illustrations and dialogue balloons.

Discuss the origins of words with your child. Latin and Greek influences are most common. For example, cent in money or century means 100 and comes from the Latin word centum. Many dictionaries list word origins.

Play charades with your child using spelling words. Each guess must be spelled out.

Review the Writing Process:

1) prewriting and brainstorming
2) first (or rough) draft
3) revision
4) proofreading
5) publish final edited copy

Have your child write a classified ad using spelling words. Encourage him/her to list what the job involves and the qualifications needed.